CRITICAL ISSUES IN
EDITING EXPLORATION TEXTS

The papers in this collection deal with a cultural problem central to the study of the history of exploration: the editing and transmission of the texts in which explorers relate their experiences. The papers chart the transformation of the study of exploration writing from the genres of national epic and scientific reportage to the genre of cultural analysis. As well, they reflect on ongoing changes in our ideas about editorial procedures, literary genres, and cultural appropriation.

The volume begins with a paper by David Henige, who confronts the classic editorial problems associated with the writings of Christopher Columbus. Luciano Formisano, studying Amerigo Vespucci, illustrates the technical problems associated with transmission. David and Alison Quinn examine Richard Hakluyt's Discourse on Western Planting (1584). I.S. MacLaren investigates the publication, in the nineteenth century, of field notes by Canadian artist Paul Kane. Helen Walliss paper looks at the institutionalization of 'exploration writing' in the activities of the great publication societies. Finally, in a paper that throws into question assumptions about textuality that would have seemed unassailable three decades ago, James Lockhart examines the textual editing of Nahuatl versions of the conquest of Meso-America.

(Conference on Editorial Problems)

GERMAINE WARKENTIN is a professor of English at Victoria College, University of Toronto.

CRITICAL ISSUES IN EDITING EXPLORATION TEXTS

Papers given at the twenty-eighth annual
Conference on Editorial Problems
University of Toronto
6–7 November 1992

EDITED BY
GERMAINE WARKENTIN

University of Toronto Press
Toronto Buffalo London

© University of Toronto Press 1995
Toronto Buffalo London

Reprinted in paperback 2014

ISBN 978-0-8020-0694-3 (cloth)
ISBN 978-1-4426-5503-4 (paper)

Printed on acid-free paper

Canadian Cataloguing in Publication Data

Conference on Editorial Problems (28th : 1992 :
University of Toronto)
Critical issues in editing exploration texts :
papers given at the twenty-eighth annual Conference
on Editorial Problems, University of Toronto, 6–7
November 1992
ISBN 978-0-8020-0694-3 (bound)
ISBN 978-1-4426-5503-4 (pbk.)

1. Discoveries in geography – Sources – Congresses.
2. Manuscripts – Editing – Congresses.   3. Criticism,
Textual – Congresses.   I. Warkentin, Germaine,
1933–   II. Title.

PN162.C64 1992   808'.06691   C94-932832-4

University of Toronto Press acknowledges the
financial assistance to its publishing program of the
Canada Council and the Ontario Arts Council.

CONTENTS

Notes on Contributors   vii

Introduction   ix

Tractable Texts: Modern Editing
   and the Columbian Writings
   David Henige   1

Editing Italian Sources for the History of Exploration
   Luciano Formisano   36

The Editing of Richard Hakluyt's
   "Discourse of Western Planting"
   D. B. and Alison Quinn   53

The Metamorphosis of Travellers into Authors:
   The Case of Paul Kane
   I. S. MacLaren   67

The Great Publication Societies
   Helen Wallis   108

A Double Tradition: Editing Book Twelve
   of the Florentine Codex
   James Lockhart   125

Members of the Conference   149

NOTES ON CONTRIBUTORS

DAVID HENIGE is African Studies Bibliographer, Memorial Library, University of Wisconsin, Madison. He is the author of, among other works, *The Chronology of Oral Tradition: Quest for a Chimera* (1974), *Oral Historiography* (1982), and *In Search of Columbus: The Sources for the First Voyage* (1991), and is founding editor of the journal *History in Africa*.

LUCIANO FORMISANO is Professor of Romance Philology, University of Bologna. He is the editor of Amerigo Vespucci, *Lettere di viaggio* (1985), *La Destructioun de Rome* (1981; 1990), and (with Theodore J. Cachey Jr.), *The History of the Discovery of the New Indian Islands of the Canaries* (1989).

DAVID BEERS QUINN is Professor Emeritus of Modern History, University of Liverpool. He is the author or editor, among many other works, of *The Hakluyt Handbook* (1974), *England and the Discovery of America 1481–1620* (1974), and *Explorers and Colonists: America 1500–1625* (1990). ALISON QUINN, who died in 1993, won the award of the Society for Indexers for her new index to the facsimile edition of Richard Hakluyt's *Principal Navigations* (1589). With D. B. Quinn she was co-editor of *The English New England Voyages, 1602–08* (1983), and with D. B. Quinn and Susan Hillier co-editor of the five-volume *New American World: A Documentary History of North America to 1612* (1979).

I. S. MACLAREN is Associate Professor (Canadian Studies/English), University of Alberta, Edmonton. He is the author of many essays on Canadian exploration and travel writing, and edited for publication the autograph text of Paul Kane's field notes, "'I came to rite thare portraits': Paul Kane's Journal of his Western Travels, 1846–48," *The American Art Journal* 21.2 (Spring, 1989), 6–88.

HELEN WALLIS died in 1995. She had retired in 1986 from her position as Map Librarian first of the British Museum and then the British Library. She was Honorary Vice-President of the Royal Geographical Society and President of the International Map Collectors' Society.

Among her many publications are *Carteret's Voyage Round the World 1766–69* (1965), *The Maps and Text of the Boke of Idrography presented by Jean Rotz to Henry VIII* (1981), and *Cartographical Innovations: An International Handbook of Mapping Terms to 1900* (1987).

JAMES LOCKHART is Professor of History at the University of California, Los Angeles. He is the author of *Spanish Peru 1532–60* (1968), *The Men of Cajamarca: A Social and Biographical Study of the First Conquerors of Peru* (1972), *Nahuas and Spaniards: Postconquest Central Mexican History and Philology* (1991), and *The Nahuas After the Conquest: A Social and Cultural History of the Indians of Central Mexico, Sixteenth Through Eighteenth Centuries* (1992). He has also collaborated on several Nahuatl philological publications.

GERMAINE WARKENTIN is Professor of English, Victoria College, University of Toronto. She is the author of a number of essays on Renaissance and early Canadian literature, and is the editor of *Canadian Exploration Literature: An Anthology* (1993). She is currently editing for publication the library catalogue of the Sidney family of Penshurst Place, Kent (ca. 1665) and is beginning an edition of the narratives of Pierre-Esprit Radisson.

INTRODUCTION

The papers assembled in this twenty-eighth volume of proceedings of the Conference on Editorial Problems deal with a topic — exploration writing — which would have been treated very differently had it been addressed in our first conference in 1965. Indeed, each of them, from one perspective or another, makes that difference its subject of study. I refer of course to the translation of the study of exploration history and its writings from the genres of national epic and/or scientific reportage, to those of cultural analysis. This process, already in progress in the decade before the commemoration of the Columbus Quincentenary in 1992 (of which this volume is part) came to a climax during that year, as almost all the assumptions behind the European expansion of the fifteenth and twentieth centuries were fiercely interrogated and in many cases repudiated.

With this interrogation in mind, the conference of 1992 focused on the specific problems posed by the *texts* in which European expansion was recorded: their creation, transmission, re-writing, translation, editing, and later dissemination and re-publication. In arranging the papers for publication, I have placed them in an order which reflects — and reflects on — this process, one which as well as changing our understanding of exploration texts, is also part of the current transformation of our concepts of editorial procedure, of literary genre, and of cultural appropriation.

We begin with David Henige, who confronts the classic editorial problems inherent in the textual history of the writings of Columbus himself. The specifically philological issues implicit here as well as in the texts considered in the other papers are raised by Luciano Formisano in a study of the particular case of the writings of Amerigo Vespucci, not only as they stand in the available manuscripts but in terms of what can be determined about their original state from their rapid translation and dissemination. We then turn to two specific case studies, one early and one late, the first by D. B. and Alison Quinn, who discuss the editing of Richard Hakluyt's "Discourse of Western Planting" (1584), and next by I. S. MacLaren, who looks at the remarkable transformation sustained in the course of their publication by the field notes of the nineteenth-century Canadian artist Paul Kane. Helen Wallis's paper then addresses the institutionalization of the process of dissemination, in a study of the workings of the Hakluyt Society, particularly as they affected the texts associated with Pacific exploration. Appropriately, in a quincentenary spirit of reflection and revision, the volume concludes with James Lockhart's paper on the textual editing of Nahuatl versions of the conquest of Meso-America, a paper which directly and indirectly throws into question almost all the assumptions about textuality which seemed so unassailable three decades ago.

In organizing the conference and preparing the papers for publication I have incurred many obligations to friends old and new, among whom I count the sixty enthusiastic registrants whose names are listed at the end of the volume. I am grateful for financial support for the conference received from the Social Sciences and Humanities Research Council of Canada, the British Council, and Alitalia, and at the University of Toronto from University College, the School of Graduate Studies, the Departments of History and Geography, and the Centre for Reformation and Renaissance Studies, Victoria University in the University of Toronto. Special assistance, for which I am very grateful, was rendered to the conference by the Istituto Italiano di Cultura (especially Mariolena Franceschetti), the Hakluyt Society, the Society for this History of Discoveries, and the Champlain Society. I am grateful to the scholars who generously served as chairs of sessions: Joan Winearls, Head of the Map Library of the University of Toronto Library, Edward H. Dahl, Early Cartography Specialist, National Archives of Canada, Bruce Greenfield of the Department of English, Dalhousie University, Frances Halpenny, Professor Emerita and former Dean, School of Library Science, University of Toronto, and former General Editor, *Dictionary of Canadian Biography*, George Lang of the Department of Comparative Literature, University of Alberta, and Theodore J. Cachey, Jr., of the Department of Romance Languages and Literatures, University of Notre Dame and the Repertorium Columbianum, University of California at Los Angeles. I am also indebted for many kindnesses and much good advice during the planning of the conference to the Committee of the Conference on Editorial Problems, particularly John N. Grant and Philip Oldfield who were in charge of local arrangements, to Katherine West and Andrew

Sheil, graduate students in the Department of English, who assisted so ably with the managing of the conference, to Ingrid Smith who typed some of the papers, to Brandon Besharah of the Graphics Department, Erindale College, who prepared the plates, to Ross Arthur who prepared the camera-ready copy, to the anonymous reader for the University of Toronto Press, and to Suzanne Raucourt, also of the Press.

Germaine Warkentin
Victoria College
University of Toronto
December, 1993

CRITICAL ISSUES IN EDITING EXPLORATION TEXTS

TRACTABLE TEXTS:
MODERN EDITING AND THE COLUMBIAN WRITINGS

David Henige

> Editing is ultimately an art that is
> practiced for a purpose within a certain
> set of historical circumstances.[1]

I

Fresh from the *Sturm und Drang* that have marked the Quincentenary, it might seem inevitable that detailed knowledge of, and interest
in, Columbus's activities have existed uninterruptedly virtually since
they occurred. Neither is the case — the former emphatically not. In
his own time, knowledge of Columbus's achievements was confined
largely to what he — aided and abetted, it seems, by the Spanish court
— chose to make known in the famous Letter of Discovery, which was
published rapidly and widely on his return.[2] Passing comments on the
first and succeeding voyages appeared in Peter Martyr's rather anec-
dotal account of the first discoveries, as well as in the writing of

---

[1] Nicholas Spadaccini and Jenaro Talens, "Textual Editing, the Writing of
Literature, and Literary History" in Spadaccini and Talens, eds., *The Politics
of Editing* (Minneapolis: University of Minnesota Press, 1992), xiii.

[2] Numerous studies and editions of the Letter of Discovery exist, both for its
Spanish and its Latin recensions. The most thorough and the most provocative
is Demetrio Ramos Pérez, *La primera noticia de América* (Valladolid: Casa-
Museo de Colón, 1986). Through an intensive textual analysis, Ramos
concludes that the letter as published is an amalgam of parts of Columbus's
own earliest report, perhaps some oral information, and passages added by
Spanish officials to make certain points known abroad, particularly that the
newly-discovered lands lay outside the Portuguese sphere created by the Treaty
of Alcáçovas in 1479. Textual analysis aside, such a conclusion is also the one
that makes best sense of the circumstances surrounding Columbus's return,
though one not particularly congenial to those who would prefer to take the
Letter as a serious — and successful — attempt by Columbus to synopsize any
shipboard log.

the chroniclers of the Spanish and Portuguese courts.[3] Few of these, however, were actually published at the time, and none of them — including the Letter of Discovery — contained enough information to excite serious interest, and certainly not enough to arouse controversy — other than geopolitical disputes — as to the details.[4]

The same can hardly be said of the accounts of Columbus's voyages that comprise the early chapters of Bartolomé de las Casas's *Historia de las Indias*, compiled between 1527 and the early 1560s, and Gonzalo Fernández de Oviedo y Valdés's equally compendious *Historia general y natural de las Indias, islas y Tierra-Firme del mar océano*, composed about the same time. The accounts of the first voyage in these works differed markedly both from other sources and each other. Las Casas's was much longer — 41 chapters and over 100,000 words. It was exceedingly — perhaps excessively — detailed and was palpably favorable to Columbus's point of view. Not surprisingly, it emanated, according to Las Casas, directly from something that he called the "libro de la primera navegación," about which he had no more to say.[5] In contrast, Oviedo was far less inclined than Las Casas to see Columbus as the hand of god made visible. His account of the same events was much briefer — say, 5000 to 6000 words — but consisted of information that complemented and contradicted Las Casas's version as much as it corroborated it.[6] The reason for this, as Oviedo duly

---

[3] E.g., Pietro Martire d'Anghiera, *De Orbe Novo* (Alcalá, 1530), xxx^{r-v}; Rui de Pina, *Crónica de el-rei D. João II*, ed. Alberto Martins de Carvalho (Coimbra: Atlántida, 1950), 184–6; João de Barros, *Asia*, ed. Hernani Cidade (4 vols.: Lisbon: Agencia geral das colonias, 1945-6), 1: 118–20; Andrés Bernáldez, *Memorias del reinado de los reyes católicos*, ed. Manuel Gómez-Moreno and Juan de M. Carriazo (Madrid: Real Academia de la Historia, 1962); Pedro Fernández del Pulgar, *Tropheos gloriosos de los reyes catholicos de España* (2 vols.: Madrid: n.p., 1951), 1: 35–51.

[4] In fact, as we can see, every effort was made to make the Letter of Discovery appear to be forthcoming without, as it were, it coming forth at all.

[5] Bartolomé de las Casas, *Historia de las Indias*, ed. Agustín Millares Carlo (3 vols.: Mexico City: Fondo de Cultura Económica, 1951), 1:181.

[6] Gonzalo Fernández de Oviedo y Valdés, *Historia general y natural de las Indias, islas, y Tierra-Firme del mar océano*, ed. José Amador de los Ríos

noted, was that he had relied for much of his information on recollec-tions of members of Columbus's crews, in particular from members of what might be called the Pinzón faction — a group that had become convinced that Columbus had stolen their fair share of the glory, and that as a consequence their role in the discovery had been neglected in favor of a scenario that pictured Columbus as unrivaled in his navigational skills, perseverance, and vision, and so in no need of aid that was merely human.[7] Oviedo had somewhat better luck than Las Casas. Whereas the latter's history was not published until late in the nineteenth century, the first part of Oviedo's work appeared in 1535 and reappeared in substantially the same form twelve years later.[8] Antonio de Herrera y Tordesillas, in his capacity as Chronicler of the Indies, used both accounts in compiling his own, largely derivative, history of the Indies which was published early in the sixteenth century, but otherwise both works languished — even though Oviedo's was in print. As a result their value was not generally recognized and exploited for nearly three more centuries.

However, between the writing of Las Casas's and Oviedo's *Historias* and their publication, two works appeared that immediately became seminal texts for the study of Columbus's activities. The first, purportedly written by Columbus's younger son Ferdinand, appeared in 1571, although under decidedly mysterious circumstances. By then Ferdinand himself was 32 years dead, and the work, entitled *Historie Del S.D. Cristoforo Colombo,* was published not in Spain but in Venice, and not in Spanish but in Italian, presumably as a translation of some Spanish-language text that has never turned up. Moreover, the

(4 vols.: Madrid: Real Academia de la Historia, 1851–5).

[7] For a great deal more from this perspective see the testimony along these lines offered in the various law suits instigated by the Spanish authorities against the heirs of Columbus: *Pleitos Colombinos,* ed. Antonio Muro Orejón et al (5 vols to date: Seville: Escuela de Estudios Hispanoamericanos, 1964 to date).

[8] See Daymond Turner, "The Aborted First Printing of Oviedo's *General and Natural History of the Indies,*" *Huntington Library Quarterly,* 46 (1983), 103–23.

intermediary of record was a certain Alfonso de Ulloa, whose scholarly and personal *bonae fides* were not very highly regarded.[9] Just the same, for two-and-a-half centuries Ferdinand's *Historie* served as the only circumstantial account of Columbus's explorations, especially for the first and fourth voyages, and during this time it was — not surprisingly — universally accepted as authentic, if not necessarily as entirely reliable. This is still the majority view, but since the 1870s the *Historie* has come under assault on several occasions. The last of these, delivered in 1960, seems especially potent, arguing on close textual and philological grounds that the Spanish source text for the work was not an independent work by Ferdinand at all, but a castoff draft of the relevant portions of Las Casas's *Historia*.[10]

Finally, in 1825 there was published the undoubted centrepiece for studies of the first voyage. It was, or professed to be, a copy of a log or journal of this voyage, and was cast in the form of quotidian entries covering the entire trip from the departure from Palos to the return there some seven months later. Yet unfortunately it was not quite a log, since it was in the hand of Bartolomé de las Casas and was professedly 80% — and perhaps 100% — paraphrase, and apparently derived from some now lost exemplar, although Las Casas never quite said as much.[11] This manuscript had been discovered in the archives of the Duque del Infantado in the early 1790s by Martín Fernández de Navarrete, who had been commissioned by the Spanish government to collect, edit, and publish the available materials documenting early Spanish overseas expansion. When Las Casas's history was at last published in 1875/76, it became all too clear that this document, commonly known nowadays as the *diario*, was in fact the "libro de la

---

[9] E.g., Juan José Arrom, "Fray Ramón Pané, Discoverer of the Taíno People," in *Amerindian Images and the Legacy of Columbus*, ed. René Jara and Nicholas Spadaccini (Minneapolis: University of Minnesota Press, 1992), 266–71.

[10] Alejandro Cioranescu, *Primera biografía de C. Colón. Fernando Colón y Bartolomé de las Casas* (Tenerife: Aula de Cultura de Tenerife, 1960).

[11] For details see David Henige, *In Search of Columbus: The Sources for the First Voyage* (Tucson: University of Arizona Press, 1991), *passim*, and the sources cited there.

primera navegación" to which Las Casas had alluded. From all appearances, he had at some point (the date is in dispute) copied some other text as an *aide-mémoire*, probably a tactic he employed frequently as he went about compiling his *Historia* over a thirty-year period, for in the *Historia* are numerous references to, and extracts and abstracts of, texts not otherwise available. The *diario* itself is only about 55,000 words long, or about one-half the length of Las Casas's derivative companion account in the *Historia*. The excess results from Las Casas's well-known penchant for discursive prolixity, endless moralizing, and frequent dipping into texts from Classical Antiquity and the Church fathers. The question then must arise: to what extent, if any, did Las Casas concomitantly embellish his source text in the process of creating the *diario*? Or, to put it another way, could it be that his source text was only one-half as long as the *diario* turned out to be? While largely unanswerable, the question is by no means irrelevant, because it forces us to consider treating this aspect of the *diario*'s creation contextually and within the framework of Las Casas's demonstrated rewriting technique in closely related instances.[12]

By the end of the nineteenth century then, there existed in the public domain all four major sources for Columbus's life and activities. Of these the *diario* is universally esteemed as the most important. It is the most detailed, of course, but has the additional advantage of being the most primary of the sources as well — however removed, still closer to any notional unadorned shipboard log (if that ever existed) than any other known source. Under ordinary circumstances, Ferdinand's biography would naturally be regarded as exceedingly valuable but, as we have seen, its authenticity labors under certain troubling handicaps. Las Casas's accounts of Columbus's activities in his *Historia*, whether of the first or of later voyages, are both derivative and hybrid — it is always challenging to distinguish Las Casas's own subliminal testimony from that of his sources, even when he claims to be quoting. If anything, Las Casas's account serves as a test of his own

---

[12] See David Henige, "To Read is to Misread, to Write is to Miswrite: Las Casas as Transcriber," in *Amerindian Images*, 198–229; idem., *In Search of Columbus*, 54–64; and below.

historiographical methods as much as it provides unimpeachable evidence about Columbus himself. As for Oviedo's evidence, it has the useful advantage of representing a non-canonical strain of testimony, but a concomitant disadvantage of lacking chronological coherence and continuity of detail. Clearly, Oviedo was forced to rely on oral testimony and perhaps some scattered written sources but lacked Las Casas's opportunity to use the *diario* as a handy *texte d'appui*. Because of this, Oviedo has generally been disparaged or disregarded by students of Columbus's activities, usually on the grounds that his evidence is hearsay. So it is, but no more so than that of Las Casas. Rather, it is its lack of coherence and perspicuity that has discouraged interest in his work. Nonetheless, for present purposes Oviedo's contribution to the Columbian corpus and its reception will be considered here, in particular because it complements the other three sources.

Perhaps, though, I should say, "other four sources," since a fifth source has very recently come to light — a copy book, dating probably from the mid-sixteenth century, in which are several letters, ostensibly from Columbus to the Spanish crown.[13] Most important among these is another version of the Letter of Discovery and several letters written during Columbus's sojourn in Hispaniola from 1493 to 1496. Unfortunately, while there is no obvious reason to reject this newly-discovered source as spurious, there is also no incontrovertible evidence that it is genuine. Since, however, it has been published in a thorough edition meeting most modern documentary editing standards, and under the aegis of a respected Columbian scholar, and since the tenor of the documents is extraordinarily evocative of Columbus's known writing, I will treat this source here, bearing in mind that its *locus standi* is probably no better than that of Ferdinand's *Historie* — and no worse.

---

[13] Christopher Columbus, *Libro copiador del Cristóbal Colón. Correspondencia inedita con los reyes católicos sobre los viajes a America. Estudio histórico-crítico y edición*, ed. Antonio Rumeu de Armas (2 vols.: Madrid: Testimonio, 1989).

II

Before looking at the editorial history of each of these sources, it would be useful to offer a brief panoramic look at the outlines of this experience. Most obvious is the extraordinarily disparate editorial treatment they have undergone. The *diario* has appeared in at least 50 editions since 1825, whereas none of the other three sources has undergone more than 4 or 5 editions. The disparity in translations is even greater. The *diario* has been translated into many languages, including 20 to 30 English translations. In contrast, there has been only one modern English translation of Ferdinand's *Historie,* and none at all of either Las Casas or Oviedo. The reason for this latter neglect is readily apparent, if less readily justifiable. Each work runs into well over a million words, each is repetitious and crushingly tedious, each treats Columbus only as a prelude — albeit an important prelude in Las Casas's case — to dealing with the Spanish expansion onto the American mainland. Still, it is both surprising and disconcerting that the Quincentenary has been allowed almost to pass away without even the Columbian chapters of these works being offered either to scholarly or general audiences. This said, we can look more closely at some of the particulars that characterize the editorial experience these works have undergone, saving the *diario* until last. It will quickly become apparent that this history, and the scholarship it ineluctably spawned, has been lamentably, and unnecessarily, unedifying.

Ferdinand's *Historie,* the first to be published, if perhaps the last to be written, is unique among the five texts in that it exists only in printed form and only in a language that presumably — necessarily by the arguments of its defenders — differs from that of the original text. There is then no possibility for any kind of diplomatic or eclectic edition; rather, it is a matter of reproducing as exactly as possible the first edition, providing a substantial scholarly apparatus, an index, and perhaps a concordance, and unleashing such an edition onto an unsuspecting, but presumably grateful, world of Columbus scholarship.

None of this has happened, however. Instead, the standard modern edition, published in 1930, consists of a text that makes little attempt to retain the orthography or punctuation of the original edition.[14] The introduction is largely bibliographical and biographical rather than text-critical, and along the same lines, the editorial apparatus is exiguous, with little systematic effort, for instance, to compare the text of the *Historie* with either the *diario* or Las Casas's *Historia*. Once lost, these opportunities have never been regained. A new edition of the *Historie* appeared in 1992, which differs frequently from the 1930 edition.[15] Despite an entire volume of appendices, there is even less attention paid to textual issues *per se* than in the 1930 edition and very little to editorial issues. Only a few pages, for instance, are devoted to discussing the criticisms of Cioranescu, and much more to the easier task of refuting earlier, more ideologically informed, attacks.[16] In both cases the task has fallen to Paolo Emilio Taviani, no philologist and an unregenerate admirer of Columbus and his works. As a result, the discussion amounts more to a defense of Ferdinand than to a rebuttal of Cioranescu, whose case has yet to be answered satisfactorily or frontally.[17]

Most strikingly, during the past thirty years or so, far more students of Columbus have relied on the *Spanish translation* as the primary source than on the Italian original. True, there have been more of these, most published in the Americas, where the majority of scholars apparently operate, but it hardly seems possible to conduct the course of sound scholarship on such principles.[18] Needless to say, the

[14] Fernando Colón, *Le Historie della vita e dei fatti di Cristobal Colombo,* ed. Rinaldo Caddeo (2 vols.: Milan: Edizioni Alpes, 1930).

[15] For instance, in the two-page chapter (21) dealing with the first landfall, there are 29 differences in spelling, 30 differences in punctuation, 4 in capitalization, 2 in word division, and one in wording. The paragraphing is discrepant as well. Cf. Colón, *Le Historie* (ed. Caddeo), 1: 158–63 and Fernando Colón, *Le* Historie *della vita e dei fatti dell'Ammiraglio Don Cristoforo Colombo*, ed. Paolo Emilio Taviani and Ilaria Luzzana Caraci (Rome: Istituto Poligrafico, 1992), 1: 89–90.

[16] Colón, *Le Historie* (ed. Caddeo), 54–8.

[17] Even so, these few pages actually amount to the most extended effort to deal with Cioranescu by the supporters of Ferdinand's authenticity.

[18] Oddly, much recent study of de Soto's expedition has also relied solely on

ways in which the various translators have treated Ferdinand are various, always subjective, and occasionally instructive, so that the conclusions it is possible to reach by using them depend almost entirely on the choice of translation, which we can reasonably assume is usually happenstance.[19]

Turning to Las Casas's *Historia,* we find something perhaps more typical, since two complete manuscripts exist which were prepared during Las Casas's lifetime (he died in 1566). Both are dated in November of 1559, but otherwise present interesting differences. One manuscript is entirely in Las Casas's hand, while the other is a fair copy, the first two-thirds of which was annotated by Las Casas at some undetermined period, but in one case at least as late as 1563.[20] The fair copy was the first to be discovered and the first edition of the *Historia* was based on it.[21] Two further editions published in the 1950s depended on the since-discovered autograph copy.[22] The two

translations of the chronicles; for this see David Henige, "'So Unbelievable it has to be True': Inca Garcilaso in Two Worlds," in *The Historiography of the de Soto Expedition,* ed. Patricia K. Galloway (Lincoln: University of Nebraska Press, 1994); and Henige, "Life After Death: the Posthumous Aggrandisement of Coosa," forthcoming.

[19] Although it might be hard to believe, it appears that English translations of the volumes in the *Nuova Raccolta* (to which the Oviedo selections and 1992 edition of Ferdinand's *Historie* belong) are imminent. According to the general editor of the project, "[w]e are converting their modern Italian translation of the *diario* (which faces the Spanish text) into American English." Personal communication, Christian K. Zacher, 8 March 1991.

[20] For the details see Lewis Hanke, *Bartolomé de las Casas, Historian. An Essay in Spanish Historiography* (Gainesville: University of Florida Press, 1952), 33-4; cf. Isacio Pérez Fernández, *Inventario documentado de los escritos de Fray Bartolomé de las Casas* (Bayamón: Centro de Estudios de los Dominicos del Caribe, 1981), 210-18.

[21] Bartolomé de las Casas, *Historia de las Indias,* ed. Marqués de la Fuensanta del Valle and José Sancho Rayón (5 vols.: Madrid: Impr. de M. Ginesta, 1875-6).

[22] Las Casas, *Historia*/1951; Las Casas, *Historia,* ed. Juan Pérez de Tudela Bueso and Emilio López Oto (2 vols.: Madrid: Ediciones Atlas, 1957).

most recent editions, published in the 1980s, in turn relied on the editions published in the 1950s rather than returning to the manuscript.[23] Under the circumstances we might reasonably expect certain differences between the 1875/76 editions and the others, but little or none among the various twentieth-century editions. And of course in every case we should expect that the modern editions replicate the manuscripts, and therefore each other, very closely.

Only the first of these is true and even then not very true, since the differences between the autograph and the fair copy are not very extensive after all. But let us look more closely at the differences among the recent editions, all purporting to be based on a single exemplar manuscript. In order to do this efficiently, I have randomly chosen the first 750 to 800 words in chapter 48 of the *Historia,* which relate Columbus's activities on the north coast of Cuba late in November of 1492. A comparison of the 1951, 1957, and 1986 editions immediately reveals that none of the editors was able successfully to duplicate the capitalization, paragraphing, and punctuation of the manuscript itself and that they each failed in ways different from the others.[24] As a result of the conscious and unconscious manipulation of the text, there are probably 40 to 50 discrepancies between and among modern editions for just this relatively short passage, sometimes with material consequences.

The most common editorial emendations in this portion of the work, especially in the 1986 edition, have been the modernizing of orthography, especially of verb forms. Thus the antique "vido" ("he saw") is silently transformed into the modern "vío," the old "sueste ("southeast") becomes "sudeste," and "diz" ("he said") is rendered "dice." The fact that these emendations do not bedevil the 1951 and

---

[23] Las Casas, *Historia,* ed. Guillermo Piña Contreras (3 vols.: Hollywood, Fla.: Ediciones del Continente, 1985); ibid., ed. André Saint-Lu (3 vols.: Caracas: Biblioteca Ayacucho, 1986). In what follows I will distinguish these editions by the dates of publication, but do not consider the 1985 edition, as it is essentially a reprint of the 1951 text, albeit with a separate introduction.
[24] Las Casas, *Historia*/1951, 1:241–3; Las Casas, *Historia*/1957, 1:170–1; Las Casas, *Historia*/1986, 1:247–8.

1957 editions may suggest that editorial hubris is presently waxing stronger than forty years ago — hardly a good sign. All three editions, however, take liberties in rendering numbers — sometimes changing words to integers, sometimes *vice versa,* and sometimes making no changes at all. Here the only consistency is inconsistency. In one edition several words are omitted, apparently accidentally, and an aberrant singular has been brought into line by being duly pluralized.[25] In one case the discrepancies in paragraphing could mislead, since a date is moved from the end of one paragraph to the beginning of the next. Since, however, Las Casas himself did not anticipate modern requirements by providing his own paragraphing, it could just as easily be a case of moving it from the beginning of one paragraph to the end of the preceding one in the other editions. Like all emendations, the choice of paragraphing is an interpretation, and one that can have serious implications. While it might be reasonably useful for aesthetics and reader convenience, decisions such as these require that readers be alerted when they happen.

The same of course is even more true for punctuation, in particular the use and abuse of commas. Many commas have been added, and a few dropped, in the passage under discussion in these various modern editions. While I have detected no specific cases of it, it is all too obvious that the use of a comma to create a restrictive clause where none previously existed is a particularly pernicious editorial decision and one that can have serious ramifications, at least to the degree that editor and readers are at one as to the distinction between the two.[26] These decisions are inevitably made as the result

---

[25] Las Casas, *Historia/*1951, 1:242; Las Casas, *Historia/*1957, 1:170; Las Casas, *Historia/*1986, 1:248.

[26] For some examples of the possible effects see, among others, Hunter Miller, "A Point of Punctuation," *American Journal of International Law* 29 (1935), 118–23; Frank D. Gilliard, "The Problem of the Anti-Semitic Comma Between 1 Thessalonians 2.14 and 15," *New Testament Studies* 35 (1989), 481–502. David Henige, "In Quest of Error's Sly Imprimatur: the Concept of 'Authorial Intent' in Modern Literary Criticism," *History in Africa* 14 (1987), 109 n. 44, discusses the troublesome effects of the disparity in usage between British and American English.

of a modern editor's belief as to the *intended* meaning of the text on which he or she is working. At the best of times this is problematic; when dealing with texts as obscure as the early Columbian texts, it can be regarded only as dangerously inappropriate.

As it happens, in this opening section of chapter 48 of the *Historia* there are several passages that exhibit both haplography and dittography on the part certainly of modern editors and perhaps *ab initio* by Las Casas himself. The principal such passage in the *Historia* is as follows:

> ... halló un admirable puerto y un gran río y a un
> cuarto de legua otro río y de allí a media legua otro
> río y dende a otro media legua otro río, y dende a
> otro otro río y dende a otro cuarto otro río, y dende
> a otra legua otra río grande, desde el cual hasta el
> Cabo de Campana habría 20 millas.[27]

If ever there was a passage ripe for transcriptional error, this is it, as Las Casas proved. In his source, the *diario,* eight rivers, not seven, are mentioned in a similarly long, convoluted, and repetitive passage. In the *Historia* Las Casas omitted one of the clauses, and therefore one of the rivers.[28] A mistake anyone might make, to be sure, but there are other discrepancies. In one of his typical *obiter dicta* Las Casas wrote

---

[27] Las Casas, *Historia*/1951: 242. There are slight differences between the modern transcriptions of this passage, one of which is discussed below.

[28] Very puzzlingly, in his edition of the *Historia,* Saint-Lu restores this river to the text; whether this is accidental compensatory dittography on his part or whether he relied on the *diario* to correct Las Casas's apparent error is not clear — as usual there is no editorial comment. What is apparent, however, is that at this point Saint-Lu was not accurately transcribing the text he was editing. Even more inexplicably, in a recent translation of the *diario,* the author/editor has in his turn reduced the number of rivers mentioned there to seven, in effect performing precisely the opposite — but equally incorrect — manoeuvre as Saint-Lu. See John Cummins, *The Voyage of Christopher Columbus: Columbus' Own* [sic] *Journal of Discovery Newly Restored and Translated* (New York: St. Martin's Press, 1992), 126.

in the *Historia* that Columbus had noted that "it was glorious to behold" these sights — mountains, rivers, harbors, etc. — and went on to add that "I [Las Casas] also believe that it is not possible to overrate" them. Finally, at least according to the autograph copy, he added that "all this is along the southern coast of Cuba" ("todo esto es por la costa del Sur de la isla de Cuba"). Of course Columbus, and therefore the lands he beheld, was located on the north coast of Cuba. This fact is correctly stated in the much maligned fair copy edition of the *Historia*, and it is extraordinary that the editors of all three standard modern editions of the *Historia* either have not noticed this self-evident error or have chosen to ignore it, not even bothering to add a "[sic]" for the benefit of readers.

In addition to these peculiarities, Las Casas badly jumbled up this text as he transcribed it — rearranging, displacing, and merging passages throughout. And — vintage Las Casas — he omitted entirely Columbus's reference to "the men of Caniba," who had "one eye and the face of a dog," in other words, the dreaded Caribs, whom Columbus called cannibals.[29] No doubt these practices are a rewriter's prerogative. Las Casas was not, after all, claiming to serve as an editor of the *diario* as he assimilated it into his *Historia*. However, his modern editors have donned this mantle, if not always the responsibilities naturally accruing to it.

If only a small proportion of Las Casas's *Historia* is devoted directly to Christopher Columbus, a much smaller portion of Oviedo's contemporary and competing *Historia general y natural* covers similar territory. Perhaps this accounts for the deplorable editorial treatment given this work. Doomed, like Las Casas's work, to be withheld from

---

[29] Las Casas also omitted other references to the Caribs, but did not exorcise them completely from the *Historia*, including Columbus' more benign reference to them about two weeks later, after he arrived in Hispaniola. See Las Casas, *Historia*/1951, 1:259; cf. Columbus/Dunn and Kelley, 216–17, 220–3, 236–7, 284–7. For other ways in which Las Casas cannibalized the *diario* while transcribing it, see Henige, "To Read is to Misread." Another example, the speech that Las Casas had Columbus deliver on leaving Navidad, is discussed briefly below.

public scrutiny for some three centuries, Oviedo's history finally appeared in the 1850s.[30] Although at least two other complete editions have since appeared, this first edition, now nearly a century and a half old, remains the one most true to modern editorial practice.[31] Not very true, to be sure, but at least it includes much of the older orthography, as well as the long paragraphs that characterize Oviedo's (and Las Casas's) style of presentation. While two full manuscripts of Las Casas's *Historia* are extant, a greater number of Oviedo's *Historia general* are known to exist, most of them incomplete.[32] Like Las Casas's manuscripts, those of the *Historia general* are replete with changes introduced by Oviedo — and probably others. Like the treatment of Las Casas's manuscripts, this fact is seldom allowed to emerge from the lapidary editorial treatments that Oviedo's text has received, which present it as a seamless whole.[33]

About the recently published *Libro copiador* there is naturally much less to comment on in terms of the application of rigorous editing standards. Published promptly after its discovery — practically

---

[30] Oviedo, *Historia general y natural/1851–5.*

[31] Oviedo, *Historia general y natural*, ed. J. Natalicio González (14 vols.: Asunción: Editorial Guaranía, 1944–5); see also the edition of Juan Pérez de Tudela Bueso (5 vols.: Madrid, 1959). The former is a reasonably accurate reprint of the 1851–5 edition, even to the notes, while the latter is based on the manuscript. Most recently, an Italian-Spanish *en face* edition of only those parts of Oviedo that deal with Columbus has been published; see Oviedo, *Le scoperte di Cristoforo Colombo nei testi di Fernández de Oviedo*, ed. Francesco Giunta (Rome: Istituto Poligrafico, 1990). Although there are brief excursuses on Oviedo's life and work, the text itself is completely unannotated.

[32] An inventory of these is in Daymond Turner, *Gonzalo Fernández de Oviedo y Valdés: An Annotated Bibliography* (Chapel Hill: University of North Carolina Press, 1967), 7–11.

[33] One of the few studies to concern itself with the crucial issue of the signs and meaning of revision in Oviedo's manuscripts is Kathleen A. Myers, "History, Truth, and Dialogue: Fernández de Oviedo's *Historia general y natural de las Indias* (Bk XXIII, Ch LIV)," *Hispania* 73 (1990), 616–25. See as well, Francesca Cantú, "Ideologia y storiografia in Oviedo: Problemi di interpretazione e di edizione," *Critica Storica* 13 (1976), 207–46.

unprecedented in this field — prepared and edited in an era finally made sensitive to the importance of employing exacting documentary editing practices, the *Libro copiador* has been made available in a format that meets most of these. It appeared in an integral edition of three volumes: facsimile, transcription, and apparatus, the last two accomplished by a longstanding Columbian scholar, Antonio Rumeu de Armas. The edition consists of a new (and most intriguing) version of the famous Letter of Discovery, this one addressed directly to Ferdinand and Isabella rather than to members of the court. As well, there are four letters detailing events during the second voyage, for which only a few short primary sources and several brief secondary accounts had previously been available. To round matters off, there are another four letters dealing with miscellaneous events in Columbus's life between 1498 and 1503.

The transcription is carefully done, with all original punctuation observed, all interpolations carefully signaled, all contractions and all quaint spellings scrupulously preserved, and with philological and paleographical notes. The apparatus is copious and deals with both textual and contextual issues, although since it occupies a separate volume, it is sometimes inconvenient to use. This is not to say that there are no problems at all with the *Libro copiador,* but they relate to matters of authenticity rather than editing. The fact is that the *Libro copiador* carries an incubus: it seems too good to be true. After all, it surfaced over 150 years after the last important new Columbus source, the *diario,* and just in time for the Quincentenary, certainly a set of circumstances bound to draw its share of scepticism. Moreover, its provenance is sketchy until the 1980s — always a troubling sign. This probably explains why the edition has had so little impact on Columbian studies, unless we consider as well the strange impediments that the Atlantic Ocean seems to exert in hampering the dissemination of views and reviews in the field.[34]

At any rate, so far the *Libro copiador* has received little attention

[34] The only reviews to appear in this country seem to have been that of Foster Provost in *1992. A Columbus Newsletter,* no. 14 (Fall 1991), 1–2, and of Kirkpatrick Sale in *Nation* (19 October 1992), 439–40.

despite the interesting new light it casts on Columbus's activities and, more importantly, on their motivation. The fear seems to be that it will turn out to be another Hitler's diary, but the grounds for testing it will necessarily be different. As a copybook dating from fifty years or so after the correspondence it contains, it cannot be judged simply on calligraphical or paleographical grounds, but on two other criteria, one very straightforward, the other considerably less so. The first, of course, is anachronism, the most brutal assassin of forgeries, while the other is the more elusive notion of 'style.' Although to my knowledge no one has yet attempted to scrutinize the *Libro copiador* for anachronisms, there appear, at first glance at least, to be no outrageously obvious ones. There are, it is true, possibly troubling hints here and there. For instance, there is the use of the word "Jamaica" in the *Libro copiador*'s version of the Letter of Discovery, whereas it is absent both from the published Letter and the *diario* itself. This is, however, a most fragile argument from a silence that means little in itself, given the problematic nature of the *diario* and the fact that both it and the published Letter were themselves probably subjected to on-the-spot editing.

Despite the notoriously elusive and subjective notion of style, it is clear that the materials in the *Libro copiador* are, by any measure, eerily Columbian in tone and tenor, whether measured by literary or historical criteria. The constant self-pity liberally mixed with recurring doses of rodomontade mimic known Columbian writings so uncannily as by themselves to lend credence to the *Libro*'s genuineness. In particular literary studies of the *Libro* have found it convincingly authentic.[35] But, while literary critics' interest may cease at this point, historians have a further professional interest in reliability. This might explain the demonstrated reluctance to put the materials in the *Libro copiador* to historical uses, although this might also merely be a function of the delays inherent in exploiting newly-discovered sources.

[35] E.g., Margarita Zamora, "Christopher Columbus's 'Letter to the Sovereigns': Announcing the Discovery" in *New World Encounters: Essays from Representations*, ed. Stephen Greenblatt (Berkeley: University of California Press, 1993), 1–11.

It has been true, though, that there has usually been a palpable alacrity in employing new techniques and evidence to address Columbian issues, particularly, of course, to the question of the landfall.[36]

Finally, of course, there is the *diario,* whose unedifying editorial history — at least as viewed from 1992 — seems to embody the stunted progress of the larger field during the last century and a half. When the *diario* was first published in 1825, little, if any, thought was given in editorial quarters — such as they were — to the concept of preserving texts *as they are.* Indeed, very different consideratons prevailed; only a few years later Jared Sparks, the most influential American documentary editor of the day, was to proclaim proudly that his duties lay in serving authors rather than readers:

> It would be an act of unpardonable justice to any author, after his death, to bring forth compositions, particularly letters written with no design to their publication, and commit them to the press without previously subjecting them to careful revision... I have of course considered it a duty, appertaining to the function of a faithful editor, to hazard such corrections as the construction of a sentence manifestly warranted, or a cool judgment dictated.[37]

In short, not only were such filiopietistic editors disposed to give their subjects the benefit of the doubt, but they felt obligated — if they were to be "faithful" — to create such a benefit wherever they found it lacking.

While Martín Fernández de Navarrete, the first editor of the

---

[36] For some of this see Henige, *In Search of Columbus,* 159–282.

[37] George Washington, ed. Jared Sparks, *Writings of George Washington; Being His Correspondence, Addresses, Messages, and Other Papers, Official and Private, Selected and Published From the Original Manuscripts; With a Life of the Author, Notes, and Illustrations* (12 vols.: Boston: J. B. Russell, 1838–9), 2:xv. Cf. Richard N. Sheldon, "Editing a Historical Manuscript: Jared Sparks, Douglas Southall Freeman, and the Battle of Brandywine," *William and Mary Quarterly* 36 (1979), 255–63.

diario, is not so bluntly on record as to his conceptions of the editorial *métier,* he clearly subscribed of the notion that editors' prerogratives superseded those of readers. Although the *diario* was not the correspondence to which Sparks made specific mention, it was nevertheless a text that had, as Sparks put it, been "written with no design to [its] publication." In the circumstances Navarrete felt obliged — or perhaps just felt free — to emend at will, with the result that this first edition reads as though the *diario* had been written at the same time it had been published. No contractions, no old-time orthography, no will o' the wisp punctuation, no indication of changes, corrections, and additions mar its serene aspect. Moreover, Navarrete rendered the hundreds of numbers — which appear in the *diario* sometimes as Arabic numerals, sometimes as Roman numerals, and sometimes as words — only as words.[38] Moreover, lacunae in the manuscript, whether in the form of spaces or missing words, were eliminated, as Navarrete made inspired and uninspired guesses as to the missing matter. All this — in fact, every procedure Navarrete adopted — created the very false impression that, as a text, the *diario* was the very model of unblemished coherence.

Before continuing with the *diario*'s editorial odyssey, it seems appropriate to discuss briefly the physical and intellectual characteristics of the *diario* manuscript, if only to illustrate how estranged its editing was from modern norms. The text bears every evidence of having been a hurried affair, as we might expect given Las Casas's frenetic ecclesiastical, political, and literary agenda. As a result there are over one thousand instances in which he made a change — either by crossing out already written matter (usually replacing it with something else) or by adding matter interlineally or marginally. Sometimes this amounts only to a word, or even just a letter or number, but occasionally whole phrases and sentences were added or changed. In addition, Las Casas played the role of critic as well as amanuensis and studded the margins

[38] Except for a few three-digit numbers. For the issue of the transcription of the *diario*'s numbers see Henige, *In Search of Columbus,* 69–72, 85–6. The implication of the patterns of usage here needs more attention and could prove diagnostic in determining the composition of the *diario* text.

of the manuscript with about 200 of his own comments. Most of these were simply the word "Nõ, ["Nota"]" intended, it would seem, to draw Las Casas's or someone else's attention to these points when the *diario* in turn became a source as well as a text. Many, however, are geographical or cultural glosses; paeans to the Indians; or criticisms of Columbus's behavior, language, or opinions. These interpolations, and especially the marginalia, allow us a precious glimpse of Las Casas the editor-scribe at work, and lend both immediacy and verisimilitude to the *diario* text. Beyond this consideration, they are, by any *modern* standard, an integral part of the document.

But modernity in this respect was a very long time in coming. During the nineteenth century, many editions and translations of the *diario* followed Navarrete's contextually creditable pioneer effort. These were based, not on the manuscript itself, but on Navarrete's edition, so that, while many were worse, none could be better. This unhappy situation was to a degree ameliorated with the publication of the *Raccolta* edition of the *diario* in honour of the Quatercentenary.[39] By then, it seems, editorial notions of accuracy had advanced markedly, for Cesare de Lollis, the editor of the *Raccolta,* took pains to correct many of the deficiencies of Navarrete's edition. Arabic and Roman numerals reappeared in their proper places, as did contractions, unfelicitous spellings, confusing punctuation, and even many of the marginalia. In addition de Lollis took the extraordinary — and still unimitated — step of including as a sub-text those portions of Ferdinand's *Historie* and Las Casas's *Historia* that related to, or were based on, the *diario.* All in all, it was almost a quantum leap forward.

Still, the leap did not close the gap. De Lollis included none of the 1000 + emendations that 'defaced' the text, thereby still forcing readers to believe that Las Casas had carried out a preternaturally tidy transcribing operation and it would be nearly a century before readers would be disabused of this notion. Unlike the situation in the nineteenth century, emphasis since 1892 has been on English translations of the

---

[39] Christopher Columbus, *Autografi di Cristoforo Colombo con prefazione e trascrizione,* ed. Cesare de Lollis (Rome: Ministero della pubblica istruzione, 1892–4), 1, i.

diario, several of which, particularly those of Cecil Jane and Samuel Eliot Morison, have achieved canonical status. But this was hardly because any of them saw fit to continue de Lollis's work. In fact, regression promptly set in. No edition or translation between 1892 and 1976 provided as much information on and from the *diario* as did the *Raccolta.*

The remorseless fixity with which this was true is amply illustrated in the edition published under the aegis of Carlos Sanz in 1962. Sanz had a reputation as a Columbian scholar, particularly for his views on the numerous editions of the Letter of Discovery. This, combined with the fact that his edition included the first published facsimile of the *diario* manuscript, could lead us to suspect that at last there had been a breakthrough. Nothing of the kind. With a certain bizarre panache, Sanz was able to publish this facsimile with a transcription that belied itself on contact. For his introduction Sanz provided a twenty-page appreciative recapitulation of Columbus's achievements, but nothing on his own editorial tactics, which were peculiar indeed. He fell back into Navarrete's practice of modernizing everything, but went even beyond this, for example, by italicizing those portions of the *diario* that, he thought, represented Columbus's own words rather than those of Las Casas. At first glance this might seem a harmless, even useful, service, but it was more of an invention, since in many cases the distinction between paraphrased and verbatim material is not clearly demarcated by Las Casas, and no editors of the *diario* have managed to agree completely over the matter of when to use quotation marks — a handy device quite unknown to Las Casas, of course.[40] The result of this schizoid approach was a transcription that contains several hundred differences *per page* from the very facsimile that accompanied it.[41] Despite this, Sanz's edition established itself as one of the most-cited of the last thirty years. What is most symptomatic

---

[40] Henige, "To Read is to Misread," discusses the dilemma of modern editors in determining what materials in texts of this period are — and were intended to be — verbatim extracts of earlier material.

[41] Maybe more, depending on the criteria; e.g., is "Pinzón" for "pinçon" one difference or three?

in all this is that Sanz apparently never felt obliged either to defend his editorial *modus operandi* or even to address it as an issue, even while permitting the facsimile to mock his effort.

Fortunately for the progress of Columbian studies, the situation was about to change, but even the change, welcome as it was, had some minatory lessons.[42] In 1976 there was published the edition of the *diario* that finally brought its editing into the modern world.[43] Its deceptively simple title, *Diario del descubrimiento,* failed to convey its revolutionary nature, while its place of publication, Gran Canaria, ensured that its impact would be slow to occur. To this was added the fact that its editor, Manuel Alvar, was no recognized Columbus scholar, no historian. Rather, he was a philologist, virtually a term of reprobation to historians. Be that as it may, the year 1976 should be considered more important for Columbian studies than any year since 1492, and certainly more significant than 1992.

The reasons for this apparently outrageous claim are simple. Alvar's edition of the *diario* was the first to treat it *as a text* — as an object in itself of scholarly inquiry, as a philological challenge whose close study was a necessary preamble to further historical inquiry, and as an entity whose physical characteristics were interpretatively important. In other words, it placed the *diario* centre stage rather than treating it merely as an appurtenance which could be bent to the will of every Columbus student with an agenda. Happily, unlike the aftermath

---

[42] Fortunately for Columbian studies as well, the editing of the *diario* never came to represent Spanish cultural nationalism at its worst, as was true for the Spanish "national epic," *Poema de mio Cid.* The edition of Ramón Menéndez Pidal early in this century was so chauvinistic in every conceivable way that it became authoritative for more than half a century, driving out or pre-empting rival interpretations and even becoming a cultural mainstay of the Franco regime. For this see, e.g., María Eugenia Lacarra, "La utilización del Cid de Menéndez Pidal en la ideología militar franquista," *Ideologies and Literature,* no. 12 (1980), 95–127, and Colin Smith, "Poema de mio Cid" in Spadaccini and Talens, eds., *Politics of Editing,* 1–21.

[43] Christopher Columbus, *Diario del descubrimiento,* ed. Manuel Alvar (2 vols.: Gran Canaria: Cabildo Insular, 1976).

of the *Raccolta* edition, the impetus provided by Alvar's pathbreaking work was allowed to continue. In the fifteen years since its appearance, no fewer than three generally satisfactory editions of the *diario* have appeared, along with, of course, many more that have continued the older tradition of providing readers with whatever the editors wanted them to have.[44] One of the these better editions was largely derivative, being the Alvar edition *rechauffé,* but with additional historical notes by Francisco Morales Padrón.[45] Besides providing a useful increment in historical annotation, this new edition assured a slightly wider circulation for Alvar's work.[46]

But the most important consequence of this new, if still minority, trend was the *en face* transcription *cum* English translation prepared by Oliver Dunn and James E. Kelley, Jr.[47] Its importance lies not so much in the fact that it is the best (that is, most faithful) English translation, as in the fact that the editors were able to persuade their

---

[44] I would like to single out for special opprobrium the 'edition' of Robert H. Fuson, *The Log of Christopher Columbus* (Camden, Maine: International Marine Publishing Co., 1987). As its title indicates, this is a misguided attempt to go beyond the *diario* and re-create a log-like text. In aid of this Fuson, whom I regard as the author rather than the editor, surreptitiously adds material from Las Casas and Ferdinand, omits material already in the *diario* but which he regards as superfluous, and changes all verb forms from third-person preterite or imperfect to first-person present. All in all, an extraordinary performance, which has sold — and been reviewed — rather well. Now a second work joins Fuson's: Cummins, *The Voyage of Christopher Columbus... newly restored and translated* (see note 28). Like Fuson, Cummins changes verb forms and assimilates matter from Las Casas and Ferdinand, though he does the latter within (rather inobvious) brackets.

[45] Christopher Columbus, *Libro de la primera navegación,* ed. Manuel Alvar and Francisco Morales Padrón (2 vols.: Madrid: Testimonio, 1984).

[46] A survey of the electronic bibliographic databases shows that only seven libraries in North America own Alvar's 1976 edition, and ten more the Alvar/Morales Padrón update.

[47] Christopher Columbus, *The Diario of Christopher Columbus's First Voyage to America, 1492–1493,* ed. and trans. Oliver Dunn and James E. Kelley, Jr. (Norman: University of Oklahoma Press, 1988).

publisher to produce a diplomatic edition which comes as close as possible to replicating the original manuscript in appearance. For whatever reasons, Alvar's edition represented the location of Las Casas's emendations verbally, in footnotes, rather than graphically, in place — a procedure which inevitably caused some confusion and misunderstanding. To an almost complete degree, Dunn and Kelley's edition has transcended this handicap, so that it produces a text almost equal in value to the manuscript itself, with the additional advantages of ready access and much increased intelligibility. Moreover, Dunn and Kelley provide a rarity indeed in Columbus editing circles — a high degree of editorial credibility, so that readers who do not have access to the original or the facsimile need not feel hopelessly disadvantaged and unwillingly sceptical, and even those who do have such access are likely to be susceptible to Dunn and Kelley's palaeographic arguments, which, by the way, frequently disagree with Alvar. Several things contribute to this: an excellent introduction which deals precisely with those issues that such an edition should; numerous and useful notes in which arguments are rehearsed, and not always resolved; and, most of all, a wide scattering of question marks throughout both the transcription and the translation. This last circumstance reminds users of other transcriptions — including that of Alvar — how rarely previous editors have expressed doubt about their ability to fathom both Columbus's thoughts and Las Casas's hurried handwriting.

Finally, the Dunn and Kelley edition provides several other useful features that should become *de rigueur* in developing editions of texts of the *diario*'s size and scope. A thorough subject index is complemented by a concordance of nearly every word in the *diario*. This alone is a boon beyond compare for students of Columbus's first voyage, and should serve to encourage the kind of hitherto tedious textual scrutiny whose painstaking labour requirements discourage all but the most persistent. In fact, the concordance itself has already raised in my mind and in those of others questions about Las Casas's/Columbus's patterns in using particular expressions, number forms, and the like — questions that can now be pursued with some expectation of success.

Some of the factors that account for the technical success of Dunn and Kelley's edition should be pointed out in closing this discussion of the textual history of the *diario*. Neither is a historian and, although each has acknowledged predispositions about certain questions, e.g., the identity of the landfall island, mercifully these have not acquired the stigmata of being professional opinions. Then again, although it is almost too obvious to mention, the edition is the result of *a collaboration,* to which each editor brought strengths that the other lacked. While one possessed a profound knowledge of early modern Spanish, the other was able to bring an understanding of the seafaring practices of the time, as well as a long professional life in computing — hence the concordance. This set of circumstances raises the question as to whether historians, even those most familiar with particular sources, are also likely to be the best editors, and I would like to return to this later in this paper.

III

As the Quincentenary winds to an end, we see that, in the arena of documentary editing at least, not a little remains to be done to bring the various Columbian texts up to speed, despite a certain degree of overdue progress. Thinking of the matter in terms of desiderata, I might suggest the following:

Ferdinand Columbus's *Historie*:

No edition of this work, including the most recent, conforms to the highest standards of scholarly editing as now practiced. Since the *Ur*-text of the *Historie* is in printed rather than manuscript format, and therefore exists (apparently) in but a single recension, the first requirement is to produce a reprint of the 1571 edition *in toto* and in facsimile. Ideally, this would be accompanied by an *exact* transcription, if only to round out the requirements. The transcription would then serve as the text around which a suitable scholarly apparatus would be constructed. Such an apparatus would ideally be the work of several competent scholars, and would address *all* relevant questions, including the philological and comparative questions which Cioranescu and others have raised and which have been sedulously ignored ever since. It would also provide a long overdue thorough examination of the authenticity issue, perhaps couched as devil's advocacy. When this is achieved, whatever the results, Ferdinand's *Historie* can be applied to Columbian problems in truly fruitful ways.

Las Casas's *Historia de las Indias*:

When compared to its potential, the progress here has been particularly abysmal. As we have seen, no two existing editions of the work come close to agreeing, even when based on the same texts. One question to be resolved is whether they *should* be based on the same texts. With the discovery of the autograph copy, the fair copy has been relegated to a kind of quaint insignificance. The theory of authorial intent, however, whatever its virtues and defects, does ordain that, instead of using the whole of one or the other sixteenth-century manuscript of the *Historia,* editors should treat the first two-thirds of the fair copy along with the final one-third of the autograph copy as a *composite* text that best represents Las Casas's latest known views.

But any future edition, whether thus premised or not, should strive for standards far higher than any existing edition has achieved. It should, of course, contain as its kernel an *exact* transcription, whether in a clear copy format or with abbreviations expanded in the text. *Pari passu,* Las Casas's marginalia and other interpolations must be included and clearly demarcated. Recent editions of the *diario* can readily serve as a exemplary model in this respect. But a transcription is hardly enough. Each of the two manuscripts, both housed in Madrid, should be allowed to enter the public domain by being put into microform and made widely and inexpensively available to interested scholars and institutions. And, if feasible, facsimiles of these manuscripts (both, of course, many times longer than the *diario*) should be printed as well. No doubt the cost of this would be great, but surely no greater than the expenses generated by the various extravaganzas presented here, there, and everywhere in celebration or commemoration of the Quincentenary.

With respect to the necessary editorial apparatus, almost everything still needs to be done. First of all, comparisons should be made between the two manuscripts. It would be particularly important to know just what changes Las Casas made in the fair copy after 1559 and how these differ from materials remaining in the autograph copy.[48] Las Casas's sources need to be traced far more fully than has so far been the case. In the temper of his times, Las Casas cited and quoted biblical, classical, and patristic sources liberally, if not always accurately.[49] Beyond this, however, he referred to other, contemporary, materials that he absorbed into his work in one guise or another, which is not historiography as we know it, but a rich leaven of compiling, interpolating, and moralizing. Much work has recently appeared on Las Casas's writing and on his traveling, but little has yet eventuated which ties together parts of the *Historia* with Las Casas's peregrinations and their effects on his thinking.[50] A concordance of at least those parts (Bk. 1, chs. 35–75) of the *Historia* relating to the first voyage is needed to facilitate study of the ways in which Las Casas deployed the *diario* as he integrated it into the *Historia*.[51] Finally, the task that de Lollis began a century ago, needs to be completed, viz., an extended comparison of the texts of Ferdinand's *Historie*, Las Casas's *Historia*, and the *diario*.[52] Whether or not Morison was right in regarding Las Casas's *Historia* as the most important of the early exploration texts,

---

[48] As, for instance, in the case of "Norte" and "Sur" discussed above.

[49] For these see Carlos Larrazabal Blanco, "Bibliografía colonial," *Clío* [Santo Domingo], 46 (1938): 59–71; 47/48 (1938): 105–15; 51 (1939): 25–36.

[50] Pérez Fernández, *Inventario documentado*; idem., *Cronología documentada de los viajes, estancias y actuaciones de Fray Bartolomé de las Casas* (Bayamón: Centro de Estudios de los Dominicos del Caribe, 1984).

[51] For several examples see Henige, "To Read is to Misread." Another, and quite fascinating, example is the 700-word homily that Las Casas put into Columbus's mouth in the *Historia*, but which is completely absent from the *diario*. It hardly needs pointing out that the fabricated speech is perhaps the most common of all literary *topoi* in works of history, but some scholars accept that such a speech did occur, although they are at a loss to account for its survival as a verbatim record outside the *diario*. See, e.g., Emiliano Jos.,"Las Casas, Historian of Christopher Columbus," *The Americas* 12 (1955/6), 359n; Demetrio Ramos Pérez, *Colón no pudo volver. La fundación de La Navidad* (Madrid: Ediciones de Cultura HIspanica, 1989), 101–2.

[52] A small beginning has been made in Henige, *In Search of Columbus*, 31–53.

it is clearly far too significant to be allowed to remain in its present condition — a series of editions, none very much better or very much worse than any of the others, but all far worse than they need to be if the evidence of Las Casas, the most used and most abused of the early sources, is ever to be approached with reasonable hopes of success.

Oviedo's *Historia general*:

As the previous discussion suggests, a great deal also remains to be done with Oviedo's account of Columbus's activities. To date most analyses of Oviedo's own work relate to his views and descriptions of the natural aspects in the Americas, Also, as we have seen, Oviedo's account of the discovery has been denigrated and ignored, in part owing to his non-Columbian and non-Lascasian perspective, and in part owing to the somewhat chaotic way in which he organized his materials, as he went from partial draft to partial draft.

In order for Oviedo's *Historia general* to assume a commensurate place in the study of Columbus, it would first be necessary to publish — perhaps as a *variorum* edition — the pertinent parts of all the extant manuscripts dating from his lifetime. This should be a diplomatic edition as well, in concert with Alvar's and Dunn and Kelley's editions of the *diario*; from what we know of Oviedo's revising tendencies, this approach should be at least as fruitful as it has proved to be for the *diario*. And, as always, such an edition would adhere to the standard operating procedures already discussed in terms of transcriptional accuracy.

The scholarly apparatus in this case would naturally include a discussion of the importance of Oviedo's account as a counterbalance to the pro-Columbus bias of the *diario* and Las Casas's *Historia*.[53] This would require bringing the information in the various *Pleitos* into play, since several of Oviedo's sources — and emphatically their point of view — participated in the *Pleitos* process and the documents

[53] For one facet of this see Henige, "The Mutinies on Columbus' First Voyage: Fact or Fiction?" *Terrae Incognitae* 23 (1991), 29–37.

emanating from it.[54] Since Oviedo and Las Casas wrote in part to refute one another, the effects of this bitter rivalry on the resulting texts deserve attention in any interpretation of Oviedo — as well, of course, as of Las Casas. Even more than Las Casas, Oviedo tended to repeat undigested information as it came to his attention. The implications of this practice, at least to the extent that it relates to Columbus, need to be teased out. Finally, as is also the case with Las Casas, it is important to search more carefully for Oviedo's acknowledged and unacknowledged sources, since he was notoriously Autolycan in his approach to available data, a habit greatly facilitated by his status as official Chronicler of the Indies.[55]

The *Libro copiador*:

Thanks to timing, the *Libro copiador* has virtually fulfilled the various requirements for a satisfactory edition in its very first incarnation, both in terms of transcription and of apparatus. But no one single editor, no matter how much a polymath he or she might be, can provide a definitive apparatus structure for documents as manifold as these. Moreover, although Rumeu de Armas addresses the question of authenticity in passing, one feels that he preferred not to fill the role of devil's advocate too energetically. Still, someone must, and this will require dealing with provenance, content, and style. As I have mentioned, first appearances are favorable to the last two aspects, if hardly yet for the first. But first appearances must quickly be superseded by a far more intensive scrutiny. Finally, even while some questions remain, Columbian scholars must either use the *Libro copiador* or explain why they decline to. Casual dismissals of it will not do.[56]

---

[54] See note 6 above.

[55] Thus the most reliable chronicle of the de Soto expedition, that of Rodrigo Ranjel, appears only in Oviedo's *Historia,* as does the first known, and probably least unreliable, account of Cabeza de Vaca's travels.

[56] E.g., Felipe Fernández-Armesto, *Columbus* (New York: Oxford University Press, 1991), 197 n. 14.

The *diario*:

Twenty years ago it would have been both possible and desirable to write a long paper bemoaning the failed promise of the numerous *diario* editions then in print.[57] Ten years ago it would have been both possible and desirable to write a shorter paper on the same theme. Now, thankfully, there is very little that needs to be said. With the available scholarly editions now before them, students of Columbus's activities have greater challenges, and at the same time greater opportunities to overcome them. My own work on the first voyage, for example, would have been different, and perhaps more than slightly better, if I had had Dunn and Kelley's concordance at hand at the planning stages. Unfortunately, the marketplace cares not a whit about this aspect of disseminating these texts. With the Quincentenary beckoning, many more new and reprint editions of the *diario* have continued to appear, including some, like those mentioned in note 44, that offer a façade of scholarly rigor that masks what are no more than antihistorical flights of fancy.

Some reasonable hope lies in the projected *Repertorium Colombianum* series of texts, which promises to offer editions of all the Columbian writings, direct and ancillary, in the fashion of the Raccolta published in 1892–3, each volume to be prepared by both a historian and a philologist. Of some concern is the fact that this ambitious series, despite massive funding, is now behind schedule, and only one volume has appeared, that dealing with Nahuatl texts. With the more and more constricted marketplace now existing, one must wonder whether, even if the first few volumes are completed and published, they will find sales substantial enough to keep the series in business.

---

[57] And bemoaning in particular Samuel Eliot Morison's own earlier critical review of the editions then available, for nearly all his criteria have become outmoded. See S.E. Morison, "Texts and Translations of Columbus's First Voyage," *Hispanic American Historical Review* 19 (1939), 235–61. In fact, reading Morison's nostrums serves well to remind us how far the textual standards of Columbian writings have come, as well as how far most of them still need to go.

IV

In the past the Columbian texts have served as inspiration for numberless literary achievements. Already in the 1490s poems had been written on the discovery, and since then there has been an avalanche of lyric and epic poetry, drama, and fiction relating to the man and the events. In this process, *litterateurs* did not concern themselves with the texts beyond seeking inspiration there, but left that task, as we have seen, to historians, geographers, mariners, and the like, who were asking questions that they believed these sources could answer, even if it sometimes proved necessary to force them to do so.

Happily, this abstention by literary critics appears no longer to be in force. For a variety of reasons, literary critics in several fields have begun to turn to historical as well as purely literary texts. To this task they bring perspectives and attitudes that have largely eluded mainline historians. For instance, literary critics are much interested in the contemporary intellectual and cultural contingencies that produce texts. As a result, they are less prone to assume that such texts can be treated as though they had been produced by authors somehow in possession of modern views and practices as to truth, accuracy, and rhetorical style. This allows literary critics to judge these texts without the bane of being influenced unduly by contingent circumstances.

More than that, literary critics have the habit — maybe the good habit — of looking beyond and behind words almost before they look at them. And when they do look at words, they look at them very closely, in the belief that there is something to be learned from every word and its placement, and even at the punctuation, capitalization, and the like. Where historians tend to look at aggregations of words in hopes of finding factual information, literary critics wonder whether these aggregations are not more likely to be attempts to follow literary norms or ideological predispositions first and to convey accurate information second. These procedures are naturally bitter pills for historians because they can result only in at least some diminution of the direct *historical* value of texts, and in some cases might even lead to the complete destruction of a source's use for historical explanation. When the source is unique — as, for instance, the *diario* can claim to be — then the damage is all the more severe, as though hunting an endangered species. Historians, I think, resent the insouciance with which literary critics undertake this demolition process, realizing that the latter usually consider their task to be complete at the stage of source analysis. Whereas literary critics might dismiss a source with a single sneer, historians are professionally duty-bound to try to preserve the value of every source so that it can be mobilized for historical interpretation and explanation — the activities that historians tend to see as their *raisons d'être*.

Although readily understandable, this attitude is uncomfortably short-sighted, for it merely preserves an illusion. In fact historians need literary critics far more than literary critics need them. While there is no need to adopt all the methodological and epistemological approaches of literary critics — and certainly none at all to adopt the abstruse, even arcane and self-indulgent, discourse of literary criticism — there is much to be gained in understanding these well enough to be able to co-opt them into service in aid of historiographical goals. So far, it seems that any matchmaking has been largely at the instigation of the literary critics, but it is early days and as more and more literary analyses of Columbian texts appear, it does not seem unduly sanguine to expect that historians and their ilk will be influenced by them *nolens volens*.[58] In the meantime, it is important to provide opportunities for reciprocal resource sharing. While no doubt much of the Columbian corpus will always remain conceptually inaccessible, there is no reason why any of it should remain beyond reach textually.[59]

---

[58] Some recent examples include Peter Hulme, *Colonial Encounters: Europe and the Native Caribbean, 1492–1747* (London: Methuen, 1986); José Rabasa, "Columbus and the New Scriptural Economy of the Renaissance," *Dispositio* 36/38 (1989), 271–301; several articles in *Representations* 33 (1991); and Margarita Zamora, *Reading Columbus* (Berkeley: University of California Press, 1993).

[59] A useful analogy here might be with the texts for the study of the Ancient Near East, where, for various reasons — some good, some bad — historians and archeologists must work with Romanized transcriptions of inscriptions, in lieu of (in ascending order), hand-drawn copies, photographs, latex squeezes

V

Whose responsibility is it to ensure that the kinds of editing chores discussed here are successfully carried out? Except perhaps in the fields of medieval and Islamic studies, the days have long since passed when scholars trained as historians routinely accepted the responsibility for editing, as well as using, historical documents. Sadly, recent observations such as that "[a]n accurate, critical edition constitutes the most nearly 'permanent' contribution to learning a scholar can make" can be considered only a minority opinion.[60] This state of affairs is reflected starkly in the orientation of the reward system in the profession. While there may be a few recent examples of doctorates awarded for editing, they are wildly aberrant, and certainly are not the most likely launching pads professionally. This is only aggravated by the fact that many, if not most, professional journals do not review text editions as a matter of policy.[61] As things stand, even willing historians are powerfully discouraged from turning their hand to editing activities, if not as a career, at least as a handmaiden to their other work.

If this is a bad reason, there may be better reasons why historians should not lay claim to monopolizing the field of documentary editing. Since historians are conditioned to use sources as points of departure rather than as points of arrival, the psychological burden of seeing the factual reliability of a source evaporate under their own scrutiny may well prove intolerable. Historians are in danger of depending on their

---

of the originals, and the originals themselves. For some commentary on the effects of this, see Simon B. Parker, "Some Methodological Principles in Ugaritic Philology," *Maarav* 2/1 (1979/80), 7–41, and Wayne T. Pitard, "A New Edition of the 'Rapi'uma' Texts: *KTU* 1.20–22," *Bulletin of the American Schools of Oriental Research*, no. 285 (February 1992), 33–77.

[60] John M. McCulloh, review of *The Monks of Redon: "Gesta sanctorum Rotonensium" and "Vita Conuuoionis,"* ed. and trans. Caroline Brett (Woodbridge: Boydell Press, 1988)," *Speculum,* 67 (1992), 637.

[61] Such reviews often — inevitably perhaps — consist of a leaven of praise to which is added an extended list of *errata,* maybe a good thing in principle, but hardly energizing to the next would-be editor.

sources too heavily to risk bringing a sufficiently critical frame of mind to editing labors. In the field of Columbus studies, this has emphatically been the case, as most notably exemplified by Samuel Eliot Morison, who took matters farther than merely accepting Columbus and Las Casas enthusiastically at their word. He went on to criticize Cecil Jane's critical stance on Las Casas's reliability as being non-professional, by which he meant that Jane was not a formally trained historian in the Morison mould. Given such a state of affairs, it is no surprise than the very best editions of the *diario* have been executed by 'amateurs,' who were able to adopt the resolutely disinterested attitude that every editor must possess above all else. Finally, preparing a proper text edition requires years of close attention to the task, a commitment of time that historians are naturally less inclined to make given their longer range goals and the lack of public credit.

Several of the many editions devoted to the writings of the founding fathers of the United States have been planned and executed either by scholars not originally trained as historians or — and this is probably significant — by those who were, but who were unable to find traditional employment and turned to editing *faute de mieux,* only to find that it is no ancillary task, but encompasses intellectual challenges at least as stimulating and as ubiquitous as those held to be associated with teaching and conventional research, however much editing finds itself maligned by those who have never bothered to turn their hand to it.[62]

As noted, the *Repertorium Columbianum* has formulated operating procedures under which pairs of experts, one always a philologist, grapple together with the texts in a kind of tag-team match. While it is too soon to determine the success of this particular venture, its potential has already been demonstrated by the Dunn and Kelley collaboration. It seems that in such situations the whole is destined to be greater than the sum of its parts as a result of editorial synergy. The technique is illustrated elsewhere as well, for instance, in two recent translation-

[62] Adam Jones, "A Critique of Editorial and Quasi-Editorial Work on Pre-1885 European Sources for Sub-Saharan Africa, 1960–1986," *Paideuma* 33 (1987), 95–106.

editions of crucial texts for the precolonial history of the West African coast.[63] One text, first published in Dutch in 1602, has long been granted token nods by historians of the area, but has seldom been used because of linguistic and cultural barriers. The other, a manuscript version in French of a work published fifty years later in English (*à la* Ferdinand Columbus), has until now been overlooked in favor of the posthumous, heavily-rewritten, and abridged English translation. Acceptable editions of these texts had to wait for African studies to outgrow its early and self-referencing giddiness, as well as for the commitment on the part of several historians to work together for several years — and through several disagreements. Neither edition could have been published without this patient collaboration.[64]

It is fair to ask if this approach increases the possibility of the triumph of the lowest common denominator, as a result of constant compromises by the joint editors. Actually, the opposite is likely to be true, as each editor serves as a check on the other's inclinations, whereas there is appreciably less evidence that a text by itself offers the same check on the solitary editor. A particular advantage is that disputes are less often settled *in pectore*. In each of the collaborative editions I have mentioned, the editorial apparatus is replete with brief discussions about differences that arose and their resolution. These discussions alone offer precious insights into the documentary editing process.

But, whatever initiatives are undertaken, and however well they are sustained, it seems reasonable to predict that, while new openings to the Columbus texts will be gained, the validity of other textual data, once thought unassailable, will be undermined on one ground of

---

[63] Pieter de Marees, *Description and Historical Account of the Gold Kingdom of Guinea (1602)*, ed. and trans. Albert Van Dantzig and Adam Jones (published for the British Academy by Oxford University Press, 1987); Jean Barbot, *Barbot on Guinea*, ed. and trans. P. E. H. Hair, Adam Jones, and Robin Law (2 vols. London: Hakluyt Society, 1992).

[64] Of the four historians involved, one does not have a formal academic job, another was nearing retirement, and a third teaches in Africa, well away from the dangers of the publish-or-perish zone.

another. While new and elevated standards of editorial attention to these sources is long overdue, the texts will continue to guard many of their secrets zealously. Thus it would be fatuous to regard interpretative closure as a natural, or even a possible, outgrowth of improved standards of editing. What would result, and it would be no mean accomplishment, is that whatever credibility students of these texts grant them would be posited on sound critical standards rather than simply on a faith born of ignorance and desperation.

EDITING ITALIAN SOURCES
FOR THE HISTORY OF EXPLORATION

Luciano Formisano

Editing exploration texts does not, in my view, demand special
editorial policies. This does not mean that, generally speaking, the
nature of the text cannot affect the editorial practice; on the contrary,
I hope that the few examples I am going to discuss will show how
important exploration literature may be from a methodological point of
view. Nevertheless, as far as editorial criteria are concerned, the genre
to which a text belongs is less important than its textual tradition; in
any case, the correspondence between literary genre and textual
transmission cannot be an axiom. In this sense, exploration texts and
documents do not distinguish themselves from any other text sharing
the same textual conditions. The texts I am concerned with do not
differ from medieval or modern texts circulating in the same form: they
may be preserved in a single copy or transmitted in multiple traditions
belonging to the Age of Discovery, they may involve printed as well
as manuscript circulation. For many of them, the difficulty of establishing a Lachmannian formula simply depends on their being written in a
vernacular prose, although the modest quality of this prose may explain
why this genre of literature is particularly exposed to scribal interventions and polygenesis.

More important is the special effect of a wide circulation: although
few reports were actually intended for publication, many of them seem
to have circulated as if they had been printed.[1] This is the case with
Columbus's log of the first and third voyage, for which we can easily
show a prompt circulation in the Florentine *milieu* of Columbus's
friends and supporters (I will only mention Amerigo Vespucci and
Simone dal Verde, whose letters, in comparison with Columbus's

---

[1] For a survey see R. Hirsch, "Printed Reports on the Early Discoveries and
Their Reception," in *First Images of America: The Impact of the New World
on the Old,* ed. F. Chiappelli, 2 vols. (Berkeley: University of California
Press, 1976), II, 537–8.

original writings, represent a kind of indirect tradition).[2] In fact, the popularity of a work could not be argued simply from the number of the extant copies; early exploration texts were considered as a sort of instant book; in this sense, they were replaced as the knowledge of the New World increased. For instance the survival of only two copies of the *Libretto di tutta la navigatione de Re de Spagna* [*A Booklet about all the navigations of the King of Spain*], the first Italian voyage compilation relating to America,[3] can be easily explained if we consider that three years later the anthology was reprinted as the first part of the *Paesi novamente retrovati et Novo Mondo da Alberico Vesputio Florentino intitulato* [*Recently discovered lands and New World, so called by the Florentine Alberico Vesputio*]: merely a new compilation where a vernacular version of Vespucci's *Mundus Novus* brought up to date the exploration of America between 1492 and 1499. At the same time the Spanish achievements in the West were paralleled with the Portuguese navigations along the coasts of Africa and Asia, starting from Alvise da Ca' da Mosto to Pero Álvares Cabral.[4]

In any case, it is hardly surprising that some authors, driven by the need for adequate publicity or patronage, seem to have helped the multiplication of exemplars. This is the case of Columbus himself, whose letter to Luis de Santángel and Gabriel Sánchez was put in print soon after its delivery to Barcelona. As is well known, the text had an

[2] For the intertextual contacts between Vespucci and Columbus, see L. Formisano, "Tra racconto e scrittura: la scoperta dell'America nei viaggiatori italiani del primo Cinquecento," in *Atti del IV Convegno di Studi Colombiani (Genova, 21-3 ottobre 1985)*, 2 vols. (Genova: Civico Istituto Colombiano — Fondazione Colombiana, 1987), I, 199–230; *Idem*, "E ci chiamavano in lor lingua 'carabi'; l'insegnamento di Amerigo Vespucci," in *Studia in honorem prof. M. de Riquer*, 4 vols. (Barcelona: Quaderns Crema, 1986–91), IV (1991), 411–38. For Simone dal Verde and Columbus, see *Cartas de particulares a Colón y Relaciones Coetáneas*, edición de J. Gil y C. Varela (Madrid: Alianza Editorial, 1984), 282.

[3] First and unique edition: Venezia, Albertino Vercellese da Lissona, 1504.

[4] First edition: Vicenza, Enrico Vicentino, 1507; reprints: Milano, Ioanne Angelo Scinzenzeler, 1512 (and 1519); Venezia, Giorgio de' Rusconi, 1517 (and 1521).

immediate following in Italy where it arrived by the end of March 1493, only twenty-six days after Columbus landed in Lisbon. By this date the Florentine Tribaldo de' Rossi could already record in his *Libro de' Conti* the most significant points of the letter, which he had probably learned of through the copy that Gabriel Sánchez had sent his brother Juan, who at the time was a merchant in Florence. The same copy was translated into Florentine, and a Florentine version is still preserved in two copies (now at the Biblioteca Nazionale of Florence), while a third copy, the language of which is northern Italian, is preserved in a codex of the Biblioteca Ambrosiana.

Other contemporary records are the Latin translation by Leandro de Cosco, and Giuliano Dati's *Cantare* entitled *The History of the Discovery of the New Indian Islands of the Canaries,* both originally published in Rome.[5] As shown by Cesare De Lollis, the Italian tradition is not only independent from the archetype of the Spanish vulgate, but has also preserved some rather original details that are lacking there. For instance, if we possessed only the vulgate version, we would not know that the Indians fashioned their canoes out of a piece of tree trunk by means of sharp stones: this detail is preserved both by the Italian versions (Allegretto Allegretti and Giuliano Dati) and the Spanish indirect tradition as represented by Peter Martyr's *Decades de Orbe Novo* and Andrés Bernáldez's *Memorias del Reinado de los Reyes Católicos.*[6] Likewise, thanks to Tribaldo de' Rossi and

---

[5] For the Italian reception of Columbus's letter, see C. Colombo, *La lettera della scoperta (Febbraio–Marzo 1493) nelle versioni spagnola, toscana e latina con il "Cantare" di Giuliano Dati,* ed. L. Formisano (Napoli: Liguori Editore, 1992), esp. 40–50; *The History of the Discovery of the New Indian Islands of the Canaries: La storia della inventione delle nuove insule di Channaria Indiane,* ed. Th. Cachey Jr. and L. Formisano, "Occasional Publications of the Hermon Dunlap Smith Center for the History of Cartography," 29 (Chicago: The Newberry Library, 1989).

[6] See *Scritti di Cristoforo Colombo* pubblicati e illustrati da C. De Lollis, in *Raccolta di documenti e studi pubblicati dalla R. Commissione Colombiana pel Quarto Centenario dalla scoperta dell'America* (Roma: Ministero della Pubblica Istruzione, 1892), Parte I, vol. I, xxv–lxvii [*Illustrazione al Documento II*], esp. lv.

the Florentine version of Columbus's letter we know that the Indians customarily adorned their pointed sticks or arrows with plumage, or, as Tribaldo puts it, with "a sort of porcupine quill."[7] Finally, in the Italian version that Hannibal Ianuarius sent from Barcelona to Milan,[8] we are told of an island "in la quale abitavano gente olivastre" [which was inhabited by people with olive complexion], where "olivastre" [with olive complexion] is a detail that only recurs in the *Log*, for instance:[9]

D'ellos se pintan de prieto, y < d' > ellos son de la color de los canarios (12 October)
some of them are painted black and some are of the same colour as the Canary Islanders

ellos ninguno prieto, salvo de la color de los canarios (13 October)
none of them black, but of the same colour as the Canary Islanders

The influence of an oral tradition cannot explain these three instances, though this tradition cannot be excluded at least when the alleged authorial intervention is confined to only one version. A good instance of authorial intervention is, however, shown by Vespucci's letter to Piero Soderini (Lisbon 1504). Besides a contemporary Florentine edition, the text has also been preserved in three manuscripts: the so-called "Coralmi copy," which, though dating back to the beginning of the seventeenth century, reproduces a very good exemplar of 1505, and two other copies of the beginning of the sixteenth century,

---

[7] See *Scritti di Cristoforo Colombo*, 124, Critical Apparatus.
[8] Text in *Raccolta di documenti e studi*, Parte III, vol. I [*Documenti diplomatici*], 1893, 141–2 (repr. in *Nuovo Mondo. Gli Italiani. 1492–1565*, ed. P. Collo e P.L. Crovetto (Torino: Einaudi, 1991), 598–9.
[9] Cited from Cristóbal Colón, *Textos y documentos completos*. Prólogo y notas de C. Varela, third edition (Madrid: Alianza Editorial, 1992).

in one of which (the so-called "Amoretti copy," now at the Library of Congress) the innovations are of such an extent that the copy could be better defined as a rearrangement.[10] In quite a few instances the rearrangement contains some details which show the hand of the author himself. Just one example:[11]

Vulgate version

>In questo luogo riscattammo 150 perle, che ce le detton per un sonaglio, et alcun poco d'oro, che ce lo davano di grazia
>
>*in this place we acquired 150 pearls, which they gave us for a bell, and a bit of gold, which they gave us as a gift*

Amoretti version

>chome solavamo donare delle nostre chose, fu che demo a uno una *maniglia* di sonagli, e parvegli che gli facessimo sì gran dono, che ci donò 150 perle grosse chome ceci, ed erano belle e buone (pure chualchuna mescholata chativa); e dettonci qualche poco d'oro che avevano, di gratia di darcene e che noi n'acetasimo, benché noi non ci facavamo pregare
>
>*as we customarily presented some things of ours, it happened that we presented one of them with a bracelet of bells, which he considered a gift rich enough to give us 150 pearls as big as beans, beautiful and good (though some of them were bad); and they gave us a little bit of gold they had as a gift, urging us to accept, though we did not need any persuading*

Not only is the textual expansion very clever, but a scribal intervention is excluded by the word *maniglia*, which, according to its meaning ("bracelet"), has to be considered as a loan-word from Spanish or Portuguese. As for Columbus's first letter, we detect here the presence

---

[10] For the textual tradition of this letter, see Amerigo Vespucci, *Lettere di viaggio*, ed. L. Formisano (Milano: Arnoldo Mondadori, 1985), 163–77.

[11] Vespucci's Italian texts are quoted from the critical edition (see n. 10); in the present instance the English translation is mine.

of a new text, the configuration of which we are not able to specify, but which belongs to the author himself, even if the editor's responsibility can only concern the textual configuration of a definite archetype. Therefore it will be enough to gather any alleged authorial interventions in a separate apparatus or in a special appendix.

And now the problem of the *restitutio textus* itself. The modest literary value of many Italian exploration texts has often been considered a justification for avoiding the usual editorial procedures. Until a few years ago, the editorial task undertaken by Guglielmo Berchet for the *Raccolta Colombiana*[12] was unique, though it could not be compared with the scholarly investigation which forty years later was to lead to the critical edition of Marco Polo provided by Luigi Foscolo Benedetto.[13] Indeed Berchet was above all an archivist, and until recently Italian exploration literature was considered a special "reserve" for scholars more concerned with content than with form. The case of Vespucci is typical, although the traditional parallelism between Amerigo and Columbus could also be extended to the editorial question, since for Vespucci too the editorial task has been considered as a sociopolitical rather than a scholarly opportunity. Yet there is a great difference, for in the case of Vespucci the need for a critical edition has traditionally been tied to the problem of attribution, with the aggravating circumstance that Vespucci's modern editors could not rely on De Lollis's philological competence. Indeed, we can say that the solution proposed by Alberto Magnaghi in 1924 is the most anti-philological that can be conceived.[14] According to the Italian geographer, among the texts ascribed to Vespucci both the *Mundus Novus* and the letter to Piero Soderini (usually cited as *Lettera* [Letter]) are supposedly forgeries.

---

[12] See *Raccolta di documenti e studi,* Parte III, vol. I [*Narrazioni sincrone*] and II [*Documenti diplomatici*], 1893.

[13] See Marco Polo, *Il Milione,* prima edizione integrale a cura di L.F. Benedetto (Firenze: Olschki, 1928).

[14] See A. Magnaghi, *Amerigo Vespucci. Studio critico, con speciale riguardo ad una nuova valutazione delle fonti e con documenti inediti tratti dal Codice Vaglienti (Riccardiano 1910),* 2 vols. (Roma: Treves, 1924, 2nd ed. 1926).

What is fundamental is the celebrative character of the two texts, the only ones which were published when the Navigator was still alive[15] and in which Amerigo could directly rival Columbus in the number of voyages and in the priority of his landing on the mainland. In any case, according to Magnaghi himself, it is very difficult to believe that Vespucci, the future *piloto mayor* of Spain, would have been responsible for the incongruities, the platitudes, the downright errors in geography that mar the *Mundus Novus* and above all the *Lettera*. Whence Magnaghi's idea of a double falsification: initiated with the *Mundus Novus,* the presumed Latin version of a lost Vespucci text, and complemented by the letter to Piero Soderini. In the *Lettera* the assemblage of already known materials, derived from Vespucci's "familiar" letters to Lorenzo di Pierfrancesco de' Medici and from travel literature, reproduces and extends the scope of the procedures already used in putting together the *Mundus Novus,* which is itself used to advantage in the compilation. As I have shown in my critical edition, source criticism reveals a semiotic operation considerably more complex than the forgery presupposed by Magnaghi, while the congruence of the printed and the "familiar" letters on the stylistic and linguistic level can be easily explained if we admit that the forgery was based on other Vespucci letters no longer extant. Indeed, what remains elusive in the printed collection is basically the extent of the assemblage, though not, however, the presence of at least two hands, one of which definitely belongs to Vespucci (three hands, if we consider the authorial rearrangement of the Amoretti copy). In this precise sense, the *Mundus Novus* and the *Lettera* are texts that might best be labelled not pseudo-, but rather para-Vespuccian. In particular, we cannot accept Magnaghi's linguistic argument that the Iberianizing diction of the Soderini letter is entirely the product of an outright counterfeit, especially if it is of Florentine origin; there are numerous terms that are rare or seen for the first time, or appear side by side with few, but significant, Americanisms.

More importantly, this Iberianizing diction is not contradicted by

---

[15] The *Mundus Novus* was first printed in 1502 or 1503; the *Lettera* in 1504 or 1505.

Vespucci's first "familiar" letter, the only one which has been conserved in a multiple tradition; Magnaghi read this letter in the plain Tuscanizing diction of the Vaglienti codex,[16] the importance of which has been overestimated. Moreover, Magnaghi thinks that a forgery aimed at celebrating Vespucci is better served by a printed record than by manuscript circulation. Yet to reinforce this supposition he should have shown that the manuscript tradition of the Soderini letter entirely depends on the Florentine imprint, while the contrary is true. Setting aside the question posed by the Amoretti copy, the most reliable version of the *Lettera* is neither the imprint nor the Vaglienti codex, but the Coralmi copy. In short, to show that there is a linguistic gap between the printed and the manuscript series, Magnaghi attempts a double falsification: he misunderstands the systemic purism of the Vaglienti codex and forgets that a philological statement can be based only on a comparative study of the textual tradition.

On the other hand, on a linguistic and stylistic level, Vespucci's Iberianisms are not exceptional; on the contrary, they can be considered the most significant feature of Italian exploration literature. For the philologist, Iberianisms are nothing but *lectiones difficiliores*, the litmus paper to estimate the textual fidelity of a copy. A few examples from Vespucci's first "familiar" letter will suffice:[17]

---

[16] A collection of voyage accounts, most of them from a Portuguese context, which was compiled by the Pisan-Florentine Piero Vaglienti (1438–1514); description by L. Formisano in *Due mondi a confronto (1492–1728). Cristoforo Colombo e l'apertura degli spazi,* ed. G. Cavallo, 2 vols. (Roma: Istituto Poligrafico e Zecca dello Stato, 1992), II, 658–61.

[17] Iberianisms are italicized; the translation is by David Jacobson from *Letters from a New World. Amerigo Vespucci's Discovery of America,* edited and with an introduction by L. Formisano, foreword by G. Wills (New York: Marsilio, 1992). The text is based on manuscript R (Firenze, Biblioteca Riccardiana, 2112 bis). Manuscripts quoted in the critical apparatus: G = Firenze, Biblioteca Nazionale Centrale, Galileiano 292: K = Washington, Library of Congress, Hans Peter Kraus Collection of Hispanic American Manuscripts, 118; V = Firenze, Biblioteca Riccardiana, 1910 (Codice Vaglienti); W = Washington, Library of Congress, Miscellaneous Manuscript Collection, 2201.

(1) vedemmo segnali certissimi che la *terra adentro* era abitata*

we saw quite definite signs that the interior land was inhabited

> *segnali... abitata: sengni più adrento di terra abbitata K; adentro era: era dentro V; adentro: *omiserunt* GW, là drento P

(2) Navigando per el mezzodì a lungo di costa, vedemmo *salir* della terra due grandissimi *rii*, o fiumi*

Sailing southward along the coast, we saw two very large rios, or rivers, issuing out of the land

> *salir: uscire GPVW; rii o: *omiserunt* GKVW

Compare with:

(2a) ordinate nostre barche, e posto *mantenimento* in esse per IIII dì, con XX uomini bene armati ci mettemmo per el *rio*, e per forza di remi navigammo per esso *al piè di* II dì, *opera di* XV leghe*

having readied our boats, laden with four days' provisions, we embarked on the river with twenty well-armed men. We navigated this river with oars <about> fifteen leagues in nearly two days

> *mantenimento: vettovaglie GW vetovagla V, fornimento K; rio: fiume GKW; per esso al piè di: presso GW, per esi V, in K; opera: circa GW, apiè di K

(3) la prima terra che noi trovammo essere abitata fu una isola che distava dalla linea equinoziale X gradi; e quando fummo *giunti con* essa, vedemmo gran gente alla *origlia* del mare*

the first land we found to be inhabited was an island ten degrees from the equator; and when we were near it we saw a host of people on the shore

> *giunti: gunto? K; con: a GKW; origlia: cima G, riva KVW, proda P

Compare with:

(3a) vedemmo alla *origlia* del mare oltregran *poblazion**
We... saw a <very> large village by the shore
*origlia: riva GPVW, *omisit* K; poblazion: populazione GPVW, *omisit* K

These few instances are sufficient to show the importance of a complete
collatio codicum. In fact, in many cases the existence of a *lectio
difficilior* is the only means to counterbalance the difficulty of establishing a Lachmannian formula or the proliferation of equivalent
readings.

Of course, as concerns the *restitutio*, the editor should refrain
from proposing a grammatical regularity which, in fact, could not have
existed. The Iberianizing language of Italian travel literature cannot be
defined as a *lingua franca* or a pidginized variety. For instance, if we
refer to example 3a, we find that in four manuscripts the lexical reply
to the loan-word *poblazion* is *populazione*, which is also an Iberianism,
but only from the semantic point of view (the Italian word corresponding to Spanish *población* is *villaggio*). As a matter of fact, in the same
text there are four more occurrences in which *populazione* is documented in the entire tradition, while *populazione* is the word we find
in Vespucci's extant letters, including the Soderini letter. But this is not
all: according to Zaccaria's and Beccaria's lexical inventories,[18]
populazione or *popolazione* is a very frequent Iberianism, while
poblazion is a ἅπαξ λεγόμενον.

One more instance from Vespucci's first "familiar" letter:

mi parti' con II caravelle a' XVIII di maggio del 1499 per
andar a *discobrir* a la parte dell'*osidente* per la via de *la mar
Ozeana*

---

[18] See E. Zaccaria, *L'elemento iberico nella lingua italiana* (Bologna: Cappelli,
1927, repr. Sala Bolognese: Forni, 1981). See also G.L. Beccaria, *Spagnolo*

I departed with two caravels on 18 May 1499 to go off and make discoveries in the western regions by way of the Ocean Sea

Of course, *osidente* and *Ozeana* (instead of *o(c)cidente* and *Oceana*) are phonetic Iberianisms and the graphs *s* and *z* are scribal attempts at reproducing the sound of the Spanish *c*, which in contemporary Spanish was still pronounced as *z*, while in southern Spanish it had evolved into *s*. Notwithstanding, in the same text I find *occidente*, which is the usual form in Vespucci's letters, where the alternative between *c* and *s* or *z* is documented even in loan-words: thus, we find *azetto* "balsam" (as compared with the Spanish *aceite*), but *acercarsi*, not *asercarsi* or *azercarsi* (that is *acercarse*: "già el sole s'andava acercando allo equinozio" [the sun was already approaching the equinox]). Accordingly, in the Soderini letter *accertare* and *asertare* can alternate in the same context:[19]

> per le molte frecce che ci mettevano nelli battelli, nessuno *asertava* di pigliare l'arme. Pure disparammo loro 4 tiri di bombarda, e non *accertorono* a nessuno*
>
> *despite all the many arrows they were shooting into the boats, no one managed to pick up their weapons. Yet we fired four charges of mortar at them, and... none of the shots hit anyone*
>
>> *asertava di: no si poteva riparare per A; asertava: accertava S, s'asichurava V; accertorono: cholsono A, accettorono C, tochonno V

e spagnoli in Italia. Riflessi ispanici sulla lingua italiana del Cinque e del Seicento (Torino: Giappichelli, 1968, repr. 1985).
[19] Abbreviations: A = Washington, Library of Congress, Hans Peter Kraus Collection of Hispanic American Manuscripts, 119 ("Amoretti copy"); C = Firenze, Biblioteca Nazionale Centrale, II.IV.509 ("Coralmi copy"); S = Firenze, Biblioteca Nazionale Centrale, B.R. 192 (the imprint) V: see n. 17.

Compare with:

> non ne potemmo pigliare piu che dua, che fu per *acerto*
> (*ibid.*)
> *we were not able to take more than two of them, and them*
> *only by chance.*

The case of Vespucci is not unique. In fact, quite similar instances could be found in the textual tradition of many other Italian exploration texts. However, we have here two different, though parallel, questions: a linguistic one, concerning the degree of consistency of Vespucci's Iberianizing prose, and a philological one, concerning the editorial procedures to adopt in the case of textual variations. As regards the linguistic question, I can only reiterate that a comparative examination of Italian exploration texts reveals a number of phonetic and lexical inconsistencies, so that the Iberianizing language of such texts cannot be assimilated to a *lingua franca*. The original linguistic context might be symbolized by the following instance from the *Lettera*:

> *sozobrammo* con li battelli molte delle loro almadie, o canoè
> che cosí le chiamano*
> *we sank many of their almadias, or canoes, as they call*
> *them, with our boats*
>   *sozobrammo: sotto braccio AC, mandamo V.

Compare with:

> ebbono tanto tormento di mare... che *mandò sottosopra*
> cinque delle loro navi (Letter II)
> *they met with so turbulent a sea... that it capsized five of*
> *their ships*

It is true that Vespucci's second "familiar" letter is transmitted only in the Tuscanizing Vaglienti codex, yet here the alternative concerns two lexical forms that might have occurred at the same time at two different linguistic levels; the loan-word *sozobrare,* compared with the Spanish *sozobrar*, the Portuguese *soçobrar* (mod. Port. *sossobrar*); the Italian adaptation *mettere sottosopra*, a poor translation in which *sottosopra* reproduces the phonetic pattern of the Iberian word.

As concerns the philological question, I have already pointed out the equivalence between Iberianisms and *lectiones difficiliores*: whatever the Lachmannian formula or the base manuscript might be, the editor has no choice: an Iberianism is a *lectio difficilior* and as such it belongs to the original text, even if the editor refrains from any linguistic reconstruction (as shown by the occurrence of *asertare* and *accertare* at the same time not only in the same manuscript, but in the same text and side by side). In this precise sense, the path to follow is a de-Italianization only where transmitted evidence is available to support Iberianization: that is the path proposed by Tuulio Tallgren in the case of the de-Tuscanization of the lyrics of the Sicilian School.[20]

Leaving aside this particular point, it seems to me that the editor has to assume a conservative attitude. Let me quote one more passage from the letter to Piero Soderini:

> tenavamo un reggimento del re, che ci mandava che qualunche delle navi che si perdesse della flotta o del suo capitano, fussi a tenere nella terra che el viaggio passato discoprimmo, in un porto che li ponemmo nome la *Badia di Tutti e' Santi*
>
> *we had an order from the king commanding that, should any ship lose its fleet or the captain, it should head toward the land that we discovered on the last voyage, to a port that we had named the Bay of All Saints*

The translation reads the "Bay of All Saints," as if the Italian text had *Baia*, and indeed it is evident that Vespucci is simply speaking of *Bahia de Todos os Santos;* in any case, *Badia* could be explained as a palaeographic misunderstanding of the form *Bahia*. However, both the

---

[20] See *The Poetry of the Sicilian School*, edited and translated by F. Jensen (New York & London: Garland, 1986), esp. lii–lvi.

manuscripts and the imprint read *Badia* [Abbey], which therefore has to be ascribed to the archetype itself. In short, I think that we have no right to follow the version given by Ramusio, where we find the reading *Baia di Tutti e' Santi*,[21] for to Vespucci the name might have been suggested by 1 November 1501 (All Saints' Day), but most of all with the church and district of Ognissanti [All Saints] in Florence, the home of the Vespucci family.

Of course the editor's attitude will be more or less conservative according to the purpose of the edition itself. For instance, we know that the *Libretto di tutta la navigatione de Re de Spagna* depends on Angelo Trevisan's translation of Peter Martyr's *Decades de Orbe Novo*; yet a comparative examination easily shows that the manuscript translation we still possess is neither the original text nor the copy on which the printing was based. Likewise, if the *Libretto,* or its model, is the direct source of the American section of the *Paesi novamente retrovati,* this does not apply to the manuscript anthology provided by Alessandro Zorzi (the so-called "Ferrara manuscript").[22] A critical edition of Trevisan's translation should then be based on the entire textual tradition, including the *Paesi* and Zorzi's own anthology: an operation which would be worthwhile, as it would show what the *Decades de Orbo Novo* might be in a particular stage of the tradition prior to the first printing. This does not mean, however, that an edition of the *Libretto* itself would not be worthwhile; as a printed anthology, the *Libretto* had its own circulation and audience, and it is a fact that both the imprint and the text are meant for a wide, but unsophisticated public. The imprint, then, holds a cultural interest; however, it seems to me that the impact of the Discovery demands the respect if not of special procedures, at least of special priorities. I am not suggesting a

[21] See Giovanni Battista Ramusio, *Navigazioni e Viaggi,* ed. M. Milanesi, 6 vols. (Torino: Einaudi, 1978–88), I (1978), 668.

[22] For the textual history of these voyage anthologies see L. Formisano, "Per una tipologia delle raccolte italiane di viaggi del primo Cinquecento," in *Presencia italiana en Andalucía: Siglos XIV-XVII. Actas del III Coloquio Hispano-Italiano* (Sevilla: Publicaciones de la Escuela de Estudios Hispano-Americanos, 1989), 341–60.

diplomatic edition. On the contrary, the editor has the right to correct whenever the text has no meaning, as for instance in the following passage:[23]

> [chap. I] veteno terra et descoprirno .vi. isole, do' de le quale de grandeza inaudita: una chiama Spagnola, l'altra la Zoanna *mela*. [chap. II] Zoanna non hebero ben certo che la fusse isola*
>> *they sighted land and discovered six islands, two of which were of unheard of size: one called Hispaniola, the other Juana, but they were not sure if Juana was an island*
>> *mela LP: ma la FT

Compare with Peter Martyr:

> quarum [insularum] alteram Hispaniolam, Ioannam alteram vocitavit, *sed* Ioannam esse insulam non pro certo habuit

Here the English translation presupposes the editorial changing of *mela* into *ma la* ("... la Zoanna. Ma la Zoanna non hebero ben certo che la

---

[23] I quote from my edition forthcoming in the *Nuova Raccolta Colombiana* (Roma: Istituto Poligrafico e Zecca dello Stato), V, and the *Repertorium Columbianum* (Univ. of California Press), II. The English translation is by Th. Cachey Jr. from the *Repertorium Columbianum* edition. Abbreviations: F = *Un giornale del Cinquecento sulla scoperta dell'America. Il Manoscritto di Ferrara*, ed. L. Laurencich Minelli. Milano: Istituto Editoriale Cisalpino — La Goliardica, 1985; L = *Libretto* (facsimile by G. P. Putnam's Sons. New York & London, 1903); P = *Paesi novamente retrovati et Novo Mondo da Alberico Vesputio Florentino intitulato*, Vicenza, Enrico Vicentino, 1507 (Venezia, Biblioteca Nazionale Marciana, Rari 631); T = Angelo Trevisan's translation of Peter Martyr's *Decades de Orbe Novo*, I *Dec.* (ed. G. Berchet, in *Raccolta di documenti e studi*, Parte III, vol. I, 46–82). Peter Martyr's text is cited from *La scoperta del Nuovo Mondo negli scritti di Pietro Martire d'Anghiera*, a cura di E. Lunardi, E. Magioncalda, R. Mazzacane (Roma: Istituto Poligrafico e Zecca dello Stato, 1988; *Nuova Raccolta Colombiana*, VI).

fusse isola" [... Juana. But as for Juana, they were not sure that it was an island]): a simple correction, which is also supported by Peter Martyr, Angelo Trevisan and the manuscript of Ferrara. On the other hand, we have no right to correct the misreadings which a reader might not have understood as such, as in the case of the *Libretto*, chap. XIII:

> Lo Admirante prese locinfrone uno loco propinquo a uno porto

that is,

> Lo Admirante prese lo "Cinfrone," uno loco propinquo a uno porto*
> *The Admiral took possession of "Lo Cinfrone," a place near a harbour*

> *FP = L, while T reads:

> Lo Admirante fece electione de uno loco propinquo a uno porto
> *The Admiral selected a location near a harbour*

Compare with Peter Martyr's original text:

> Ipse propinquum portui cuidam editum locum... elegit.

From a more general perspective, the impact of written reports explains the frequency of the form *camballi* instead of *caniballi* (that is *canibales*, later on *caníbales*), which is due to a palaeographic misreading of the group *in*. But we find also *chanea* and *canna* instead of *c(h)anoa* [canoe]: the former due to a paleographic confusion between *o* and *e*, the latter based on the form *canua* with the subsequent confusion between *u* and *n*. However, according to the meaning of the Italian *canna* [cane], I do not exclude that the scribal mistake might have involved the idea that a canoe was a boat made with canes.

Above all, as regards proper names, it is quite possible that a scribal or printing mistake has survived in oral communication, as shown by the *Libretto*, for instance:

(1) passorno per un'altra isola... li missono nome Monferr-ato* (chap. IX)
   they passed another island... they named it Monferrato
      *Monserrate [= Santa María de M.] >
      †Monserrato > Monferrato

(2) uno Pietro Alonso chiamato el Negro* (chap. XXVI)
   a certain Pero Alonso called the Black
      *Niño > †Nigno > Negro

(3) una provincia chiamata Curtana* (chap. XXVIII)
   a province called Curtana
      *Curiana [= Curianá] > Curtana.

Accordingly, in Alessandro Zorzi's *Additions to the "Paesi novamente retrovati"* (post 1507),[24] we find *Pincone, Beragna, Saragna* instead of *Pinçón (Pinzón), Beragua, Xaragua (Xaraguá)*; in the *Libretto*, *Oreda* is the regular form of *Oieda ((H)ojeda)*, and so on.[25]

To sum up, I do not think that editing exploration texts demands the modification of our traditional editorial criteria; what we need is an attentive evaluation of each case, a careful examination of the sources at our disposal, and a commentary rich in philological and linguistic observations; in other words, a modest but honest philology.

---

[24] In *Raccolta di documenti e studi*, Parte II, vol. II, 213–25.
[25] For a more general perspective, see L. Formisano, "Considerazioni di metodo in margine a una nuova edizione (*Repertorium Columbianum*, vol. VI)," in *Italian Renaissance Studies in Arizona. Selected Papers from the Proceedings of the 1987 Sixteenth Century Conference. Medieval and Renaissance Center, Arizona State University*, ed. J.R. Brink, P.R. Baldini (*Rosary College Italian Studies*, 3; River Forest, Ill.: Rosary College, 1989), 9–15, esp. p. 12.

THE EDITING OF RICHARD HAKLUYT'S "DISCOURSE OF WESTERN PLANTING"

D. B. and Alison Quinn

The treatise, "A particuler discourse concerninge ... the westerne discoveries lately attempted," is a document offering a number of problems which differentiate it from other Elizabethan documents on colonization. In the first place, it exists in only a single copy, and, although this is contemporary, it is not the original. That was presented by its author Richard Hakluyt to Queen Elizabeth on 6 October 1584[1] and was never seen or found referred to thereafter for nearly two centuries. The Reverend Richard Hakluyt, when he wrote it, was a Student (i. e. a Fellow) of Christ Church, Oxford, but he was on leave to act as chaplain, secretary, and, we might say, commercial attaché at the English embassy in Paris and had been there since the previous October. Although his task was technically to assist the ambassador, Sir Edward Stafford, which we know he did conscientiously, his real work was to collect information on French achievements and activity in transatlantic venturing, past, present, and future, and to collect all the information he could from books and personal contacts about the Spanish and Portuguese empires in the Americas. The objective of this was to serve the cause of the small but influential group of individuals, most of them close to the Queen, who had been developing plans for imperial expansion focused on North America, where England's only stake so far was a share in the inshore fishery at Newfoundland.[2] The nominal acquisition of an English title to the island of Newfoundland, made shortly before Hakluyt's despatch to France by Sir Humphrey Gilbert, was a token that such a movement was making headway, even if Gilbert failed and died in his attempt to install colonies in North America.[3] The practical purpose of Hakluyt's work in France was, in

---

[1] D. B. Quinn, ed., *The Hakluyt Handbook* I (London: Hakluyt Society, 1974), 286.

[2] See D. B. Quinn, ed., *The Voyages and Colonising Voyages of Sir Humphrey Gilbert* (2 vols. London: Hakluyt Society, 1940).

[3] D. B. Quinn, *North America from Earliest Discovery to First Settlements*

its early phase, to collect and convey information on French plans for the Maritimes and St. Lawrence which would serve as background information for the plan of Christopher Carleill, stepson of Sir Francis Walsingham, Elizabeth's principal secretary of state, and Hakluyt's master, to establish a trading settlement near the mouth of the St. Lawrence where he might establish a fur trade and compete with the French, who were active up-stream each summer and were bringing many valuable furs to France.[4] He did this conscientiously, though we do not have the reports he sent direct to Carleill. In the spring of 1584, when it was believed Carleill would have set out, the focus of his activities was redirected by Walsingham to accumulate materials for Walter Ralegh, the Queen's new favourite, on whom she was heaping favours. He was instructed to take up Gilbert's plans and establish a colony of settlement farther south on the coast of eastern North America as the nucleus for extensive English colonization and as an advance base against the Spanish on whom the English were waging an unofficial war in the Caribbean and Florida by means of piratical squadrons.[5] Walsingham and Ralegh became aware that, since no major mercantile interest in American colonization had yet been aroused, royal support and assistance could be vital in preventing further failures and achieving a successful foothold across the Atlantic. In the summer of 1584, when Ralegh had sent out two small vessels to reconnoitre a site for the initial colony,[6] Hakluyt was recalled to England and given the task of setting out all the arguments he could think of which might induce the Queen to support, in some major degree, the colonizing enterprise. It was for this purpose that he wrote and presented the "Discourse" with which we are concerned.

(New York: Harper and Row, 1977), 347–68.

[4] D. B. Quinn, *Explorers and Colonists: America 1500–1625* (London: The Hambledon Press, 1990), 285–300.

[5] See Kenneth R. Andrews, *Trade, Plunder and Settlement* (Cambridge: Cambridge University Press, 1984).

[6] D. B. Quinn, *Set Fair for Roanoke: Voyages and Colonies, 1584–1606* (Chapel Hill: University of North Carolina Press, 1985), 20–44.

It is necessary now to say something about the surviving manuscript. Hakluyt had to return to France on diplomatic business immediately after his presentation of the treatise, so he left a copy, or sent one over from France, to be copied by a scrivener. He must have given a copy to Ralegh, as we can trace its influence, we think, on some of Ralegh's subsequent activities, but the scrivener did not complete Walsingham's copy until late April or early May 1585,[7] and was then offering to make other copies available to other dignitaries. We are not sure precisely who they were (though we can draw up a shortlist of potential purchasers).[8] It is one of these copies which has come down to us, and is now in the New York Public Library. It was unknown to the scholarly world until 1877 when Leonard Woods and Charles Deane published it in Cambridge, Massachusetts, as a volume in the *Documentary History of the State of Maine*[9] (an area with which it had no connection whatsoever) and also Deane had a small edition run off for himself. These scarce publications gradually aroused some scholarly interest, but the "Discourse" never appeared in a modern edition until 1935 when the New York Public Library allowed Eva G. R. Taylor, the eminent geographer, to print it in her two-volume edition of the surviving papers of the two Richard Hakluyts in the Hakluyt Society series.[10] Since then it has come to be regarded as the most important single document which embodied all the ideas that were current in the late Elizabethan period regarding North America, and continued to be so in some degree or another for the next half-century or so.

The provenance of the volume is completely blank until 1770 when it was in the Library of the recently deceased Sir Peter Thompson, in Poole, Dorset. He had had a profitable mercantile career in London and had become a collector of books and manuscripts, taking his collections back to his native town when he retired in 1763. Its

---

[7] Hakluyt promised it to Walsingham by Easter, 1585. P. R. O., SP15/29,9.

[8] P. R. O., SP12/195, 212.

[9] Vol. II (Cambridge, Mass.: Riverside Press, 1877); the same press produced the separate edition.

[10] Eva G. R. Taylor, *The Original Writings and Correspondence of the Two Richard Hakluyts* (2 vols. London: Hakluyt Society, 1935).

history can be traced through various owners down to 1854 when it became part of the great Phillipps Collection. Leonard Woods found it there and Sir Thomas allowed him to have a copy made of it, which he took to the United States and subsequently published. The manuscript appeared in a Phillipps manuscripts' sale in 1913 and before 1923 came into the possession of the New York Public Library.[11]

The Hakluyt Society has for some years intended to have a

---

[11] John Hutchins, *History and Antiquities of the County of Dorset,* 3rd edition (Westminster: Nicholls, 1861), I, 66–7, provides basic information on Thompson. It appears that his library remained in the possession of his heirs for the next 25 years. It appeared in R. H. Evans, *A Catalogue of the Library of Sir Peter Thompson... April 29, 1815,* p. 15, (lot 401) (British Library 621. g. /1); W. B. Thompson, *Sir Peter Thompson's Library* (Reprinted from *Notes and Queries for Somerset and Dorset* March 1925). (British Library copy: 1902. c. 53.) It came into the possession of Arthur Annesley, Viscount Valentia, and was in the Arley Castle (Staffordshire) sale of 6 December 1852 (British Library: Manuscripts Department, P. B. I. g. 2). Henry Stevens in *Recollections of James Lenox and the Formation of his Library,* edited by V. Paltsits (New York: New York Public Library, 1951), 13, claimed to have acquired the manuscript and to have retained it for several years, being unable to find a purchaser, but is mistaken. William Pickersgill bought it (item 1080) at the Valentia sale for £29 18s. 6d.; it was later placed in the Puttick and Simpson Sale of 24–29 May 1854 (lot 474), and sold to Sir Thomas Phillipps, who gave it the manuscript number of 14097 and included it in his privately printed calalogue, *Librorum manuscriptorum D. Thomas Phillipps, Bart.* (1838–67), p. 262 (British Library copy: Tab. 436. a. 8). It was in Phillipps's hands when Leonard Woods saw it, and was allowed to have a copy made. In the long course of the dispersal of the Phillipps collection the "Discourse" did not appear until the 16th portion was sold at Sotheby's on 19 May 1913 (lot 43) and was bought by the New York booksellers, Dodd, Livingston, for $270. They offered it (according to a MS memorandum by Victor Paltsits in the N. Y. P. L.) for $2,000 which the Library could not afford at that time. A friend of the library, I. N. P. Phelps Stokes, bought it and retained it for some years but eventually sold it to Edward S. Harkness for presentation to the New York Public Library (V. Paltsits, "A Notable Gift of two American Manuscripts," *Bulletin of the New York Public Library* XXVI [1923] 255–7), where it has since remained.

scholarly edition of the treatise published, and I and my wife Alison elected ourselves for the task. This was to prepare a facsimile reproduction, a line-by-line transcription, a full commentary on its contents, together with what could be found on the provenance of the manuscript. This involved us in extensive research in England and the United States in the intervals of our other work. It was nearing completion at the end of 1989 when Alison fell ill and much of my attention has subsequently been concerned with her care, but it was completed in 1991 and has been edited so it could be published in March, 1994 in the Society's Extra Series (no. 45). The treatise is written in a clear Court Hand,[12] as used by notaries of the period. The title page indicates that it was written after January 1585 when Ralegh was knighted. The binding is brown contemporary calf, in quite exceptional condition, decorated with a gilded ornament on the front and back cover, but with no title, and no indication anywhere of its original ownership. It is therefore impossible to say with any certainty to whom it first belonged, but it is most likely to have been the copy presented by Hakluyt to Walsingham on his next visit to England in May 1585.[13] This is more likely than if, for example, it was Lord Burghley's copy, as his library is well enough known through its sale in 1694. It could conceivably have been the Earl of Leicester's, who we know was anxious to have a copy, or even Lord Howard of Effingham's or Sir Christopher Hatton's. But we have settled, with some slight reservations, on its having been Walsingham's, whose library did not, apparently, survive his death and was dispersed in ways which have not yet been established. Why the volume disappeared for so long, nearly two centuries, is quite inexplicable so far.

The volume is a small folio bound in contemporary brown calf, measuring 16 1/2 inches by 11 1/2 inches. The spine is unlettered, but is panelled with gold tooled bands, between which are small quatrefoil gold stamps. The front and back covers are identical, with a single line

---

[12] Compare scriveners' writings from "The Common Paper" in the Guildhall Library, in Sir Hilary Jenkinson's *The Later Court Hand in England* (Cambridge: Cambridge University Press, 1927), plate XX (1591).

[13] P. R. O., SP12/170,1.

of gold tooling near the edges, supported by lines of double blind tooling. The gold centrepiece has conventional scroll work, in a pattern which is found in the 1580s and much later.[14] The binding and decoration are therefore commercial in origin, and do not provide any direct clue to ownership, though it is possible that research could eventually lead to the identification of the binder. Apart from a little rubbing in the front top corner and a few very minor breaks in the tooling on the spine, it is in perfect condition. It is rare to find a manuscript of the period in such fine shape, when its contents might be expected to have been frequently consulted by its owners. The text is on good quality French paper, the watermark identifying it as being made at Noyes by Nicholas le Bec.[15]

The twenty-one chapters are set out in some detail in a contents list intended to give the Queen a good idea of what Hakluyt was covering. He starts with religion. This is not primarily directed to the ideal of converting the inhabitants of North America but to establishing a bridgehead of converted people overseas to counter Catholic claims of their successes in Christianizing inhabitants of the Iberian empires. Besides, he urged (since this was an anti-Spanish tract as well as much else), Protestant Indians might be useful as auxiliaries against the Spanish empire when the time came to attack it. He went on to specify the decline of English trade with Europe, much of which he blamed on Spain. This led naturally to a glowing description of all the possible advantages which could arise from exploiting the real or, at least, indicated riches of North America which would replace the need to import from almost any other country. The logical result of acquiring control of North America, or a substantial part of it, was to provide an

---

[14] Mr. Carey Bliss of the Henry E. Huntington Library kindly showed us several volumes of the period with the same stamp. That which most closely compared with that on the "Discourse" was a copy of Hakluyt's *Principall Navigations* (1589), priced 9s., showing it to have been bought bound (shelf no. : Folio 5437).

[15] C. M. Briquet, *Les filigranes,* ed. Allan Stevenson, 4 vols. (Amsterdam: Paper Publication Society, 1968), I, 146, with examples from 1566 to 1599.

outlet for people who could be spared from England to live and work
in conditions of great profit to themselves, while very many decayed
industries at home could be revived by trade with the inhabitants and
with the colonists.

The treatise was basically anti-Spanish and anti-Catholic, but it
encapsulated the fullest possible programme for an English take-over
of North America by the establishment of a rapidly growing population
of English settlers, under the English crown, and the not wholly
compatible objective of turning the Native Americans into members of
the Church of England and enlisting them, ultimately, in an attack on
Spanish America. At the same time it showed a practical concern for
the realities of colonization by enumerating categories of settlers which
should be taken, and detailing the equipment and supplies which must
go with them if the colonies were to succeed. There was some
ambiguity in Hakluyt's plans for the speed of colonisation. At times he
is providing for a small colony or colonies to open the way for more,
and at other times is advocating rapid and mass settlement. There was
method, however, in this as Ralegh, backed by Walsingham, could plan
only relatively small settlements to begin with, while, if the Queen
would put the resources of her kingdom behind the venture — the
ultimate purpose of the treatise being to persuade her to do so — then
large scale and rapid settlement might well be possible.

In order to reinforce every aspect of his proposals Hakluyt used
a battery of resources, besides his considerable power of argument and
rhetoric. These comprised generalizations about the defects of the
Spanish empire, buttressed by documents and narratives wherever he
could find them. He was able to cite personal contacts with Frenchmen
who knew details of French activities and plans for North America, and
details about the Spanish empire culled from the exiled Dom António
and his little court in exile in France, with occasional reports from
Spain itself and odds and ends of information gleaned by Walsingham's
extensive spy network which had been passed to him. He had collected
important French material in manuscript on the Spanish Indies, much
of which he gave in full. He had, too, important documents which had
reached England, such as a report of one of John Hawkins's men taken
at San Juan de Ulua in 1568 who had returned after many years in

Mexico and Spain.[16] He could even cite interviews he had in London with persons with transatlantic experience since his return to England a few months before. Above all, he had books and pamphlets covering a very wide range of good and bad information to cite. There was a certain amount already available in English, especially about the Frobisher voyages of 1576–8 and Gilbert's recent voyage of 1583, which he had collected before he went to France, as well as such continental material as he could then lay his hands on in his published *Divers voyages* of 1582.[17] His greatest single resource was the third volume of Ramusio's great *Viaggi et navigationi*, probably in the edition of 1565 rather than that of 1556, which he had owned for some years. He had an amanuensis (possibly his teacher of Italian at Oxford, John Florio) copy out long passages in Italian,[18] which he presented as they were, since he was flattering the Queen by playing on his knowledge that she read Italian easily, while he also cited other works in Latin for the same reason since she was proficient in that also. But he had learned Spanish in France, as well as some Portuguese, which gave him access to a wider range of published sources. And we might say that the greatest single advantage he had from his stay in France, mainly in Paris, was access to libraries and bookshops. He made the acquaintance of André Thevet and borrowed manuscripts and possibly books from him (they were to quarrel later),[19] and he had access, we do not know to what extent, to the royal library, the greater part of

---

[16] Miles Philips had presented his account of his experiences in Mexico and Spain, 1568–82, to Queen Elizabeth in 1582. Hakluyt is likely to have obtained a copy through Walsingham before he left for France.

[17] *Divers voyages touching the discoverie of America* (London: Thomas Woodcocke, 1582), a collection of such narratives and other papers on North America as Hakluyt was then aware of, published as propaganda for Gilbert's plans for his second expedition. See, *Hakluyt Handbook*, II, 461–7.

[18] *The Hakluyt Handbook*, I, 271–2. This reflects some Tuscan variations of Ramusio's Venetian practices, thus indicating the intervention of a copyist. If it was not material obtained through Florio, it could have been the work of one of Hakluyt's more recent contacts in Paris.

[19] *Hakluyt Handbook* I, 281. The relationship is detailed in Frank Lestringent, *André Thevet* (Geneva: Droz, 1991).

which had been moved from Fontainebleau to the Abbey of St. Martin in Paris. It is probable that Walsingham subsidized his purchase of books by Spanish, Portuguese, Dutch, Italian and, above all, French authors, very many of which he referred to as if he had read them, as he probably had, throughout the treatise. He often mentioned his authority by name but rarely gave precise details of his reference or citation. Sometimes he simply cited a string of authors by name. The chief task of our commentary was, therefore, to identify, translate, and track down the more obvious and the more oblique references so far as we possibly could. The commentary therefore became extensive. We also included a certain amount of explanation of why, or probably why, he took a particular line of argument and how relevant it was to his general topic. It was not our job to argue with him, but to explain the context. As someone who had taught theology at Oxford it was not surprising that he should have cited a few of the early Christian Fathers, though he gives no references to his several mentions of Jerome and cites Chrysostom from a Latin edition of a single work. He also used a Latin Bible. The Tremellius and Junius Protestant version had been available in a London printing since 1580 (STC 2nd. ed. 2056), but he is likely to have used a continental edition. His translations of biblical texts were made from the Latin and not from the two versions of the Bible available in English (the Bishops' Bible and the Geneva Bible).

In general, even though Hakluyt's citations were made to prove a point and to stress the bias against Spain or the papacy where relevant, he was conscientious enough in his use of materials from printed sources, but he did slip from time to time. He attributed to Oviedo, for example, views which he never expressed in his extensive history. And, of course, much of his material was not strictly true: it either represented imperfect information in his sources, or mythical or semi-mythical tales which had appeared in print or which he had heard and credited. The general effect of his special pleading is that of a scholarly address to a scholarly Queen. If he slipped into polemic, as he did about the division of the non-European world between Spain and Portugal by Alexander VI, or cited the passages from Bartolomé de las Casas which suited his anti-Spanish case, he was not out of tune with respectable controversial literature of his time. He never descended into the vulgar abuse of both Catholic and Protestant disputants in the intermittent pamphlet war which continued throughout Elizabeth's reign.

If he gave distorted impressions of the Cabot Voyages of 1497–1509, this was because Sebastian Cabot had muddied the waters by claiming himself to be the prime discoverer, and this was distorted again by tales told secondhand from Cabot to Ramusio and retailed by him.[20] If he appeared to accept that Madoc had discovered America for the British crown in 1170, he was distorting Welsh history as well as accepting wholly inadequate evidence,[21] but he was following the example of the Queen's astrologer John Dee who had dug up the Madoc story from no one knows where. Yet if he wanted to make a case to the Queen that the English monarch had any title to North America by historical right, this was the best evidence he could bring to the case he developed. Similarly, if he tried to convince the Queen that a northwest passage around America, or perhaps through it, would lead the English to China, he had only maps and charts, and the wholly inconclusive data from Frobisher's voyages to aid him.[22] Even when he stressed the weakness of the Spanish hold on the Caribbean, which Drake was to illustrate in 1585-6, he paid no real attention to the enormous strength of Spanish resources as a whole, which were to defy so many English assaults between 1585 and 1600.[23] His optimism, too, about the willingness of the Native Americans, living under

---

[20] See D. B. Quinn, *England and the Discovery of America, 1481-1620* (New York: Knopf, 1974), 138–46; James A. Williamson, *The Cabot Voyages and Bristol Discovery under Henry VII* (Cambridge: Hakluyt Society, 1962), 146–73.

[21] See *DCB* I, 677-8.

[22] See Viljhalmar Stefansson, *The Voyages of Martin Frobisher* (2 vols. London: Argonaut Press, 1938), where the contemporary published material is reprinted.

[23] K. R. Andrews, *Trade, Plunder and Settlement* (Cambridge: Cambridge University Press, 1984), 223-55, and *Elizabethan Privateering* (Cambridge: Cambridge University Press, 1964), *passim*.

Spanish rule, to revolt against their masters was largely wishful thinking, backed by wholly inadequate evidence. In the end, he envisaged a closed commercial empire based on the interchange of English and American produce (whether indigenous or developed by the colonists or by trade with the inhabitants) which together would render Elizabethan England virtually independent of European and Iberian overseas commerce. This incipient mercantilism was an intelligible reaction to the partial exclusion of England from commerce with large parts of Europe, even if it had very little hope of realization.

The geography of the North Atlantic, too, was very imperfectly understood in England at that time. Hakluyt was under the false illusion that access to all of eastern North America was as easy and quick as the cod fishermen found sailing to Newfoundland in late spring and early summer, while he underestimated the dangers of the West-East passage through the treacherous westerlies. His ignorance, too, of the nature of the continental climate of eastern North America, which he wrongly assumed was identical to that of Atlantic Europe, led him wildly astray on what crops could be grown in latitudes between about 32 and 45 degrees in America.

In the commentary our task was partly to track down the sources, not always specified, from which he obtained his information, and to indicate briefly where and when he was being unrealistic or simply wrong. When Hakluyt came to lay out practical requirements for the setting up of a colony, his first concern was military (and implicitly naval as he had set out naval objectives in his anti-Spanish chapters). Forts would guard the colonists from possible Spanish attacks and, though he expected the settlers to have friendly relations with Native Americans, he knew that in practice there was bound to be some resistance, so that internal defences were necessary. The specialties and weapons of soldiers and fortification experts were laid out in successive lists; then came the craftsmen — a long list necessary for constructing settlements and maintaining them — farmers and specialist horticulturists, including one to cultivate vines and sugar and such Mediterranean-style products (citrus fruits too). These were designed both for service to the colonists and for the establishment of an export trade in specified products, especially those related to timber, as Hakluyt considered that sawn timber could be exported to England in bulk, and notably, fine timber for chests from cedar, etc., while makers of chests would create a domestic industry in products which could be exported. There would be shipbuilding too and specialists to undertake it; then a list of men to provide personal service to the colonists: barbers, launderers, tailors, shoemakers, tanners, and, of course, traders (he thought woollen caps would be especially attractive to the native peoples). He recognized that specialist *vignerons* and sawmill experts would need to be recruited from other countries (he probably had French Huguenots particularly in mind). The whole set of proposals was clearly the fruit of much thought, but it was much too elaborate for any pioneering series of expeditions and settlements. Then there were provisions — "Dead victuall" — every kind of ships' provisions, and many kinds of wine, *aqua vitae*, cider and beer. This basic food supply was intended to see the colonists over a winter (we presume). But to supply future needs, every kind of edible root and herb must also be brought in the form of seeds to be sown, salads and herbs being prominent among them, as well as every kind of grain. Livestock was essential, from fowl to pigs, dogs for hunting and defence. The specialist horticulturists included "Sugar cane planters with the plants, Vyne planters, Olyve planters." His proposal to bring turkeys showed how deficient he was in effective knowledge of North American fauna. All these recommendations were for large and extensive plantations, and added up to a degree of elaboration in the recruiting and organizing of colonists which was quite impracticable on the scale he contemplated, but the prescriptions looked well and were evidence of how much thought he had put into his planning. He added an appendix of things forgotten, and here he prescribed clearly for a small, initial expedition: one or two clergymen, a surgeon and a physician, an apothecary. More of them would have been needed, especially clergy, if missionary work was to be seriously contemplated. He added bibles, prayer books, books on discoveries, and tardily, a code of laws to be laid down for the colonists. His earlier thinking evidently had not gone all the way towards meeting the religious, medical and legal necessities of colonization.

The commentary on each and every of these practical, or apparently practical, items had necessarily to be thorough. Some of them eluded us; despite extensive search in the history of brewing Alison failed to identify his "Bere brewed specially in speciall tyme." Similarly, he reported that he had been told about a gentleman in Worcestershire who had a water-powered sawmill, such as he knew was common in the Baltic countries, but we never succeeded in identifying who it was who had the English sawmill (he would have seen some in France if he had looked). On the whole the making of the commentary on this section of the "Discourse" was quite an entertaining pastime. We did take the risk of indicating which items might and might not be appropriate to the area soon to be named Virginia in the early stages of its settlement.

To a discussion of the provenance of the volume, we added in an appendix the limited number of documents which preceded Hakluyt's return to England which were relevant to his work on the "Discourse." The bibliography, too, proved quite an extensive one. The commentary could not have been completed without a considerable amount of work being done in England — in the British Library, as it became before we were finished — the Public Record Office, the Guildhall Library, the Bodleian Library. But more was done in successive summers in the United States — in the John Carter Brown Library most of all — the New York Public Library, the Folger Shakespeare Library, the Library of Congress, and, finally, the Henry E. Huntington Library in California. We had also to call on many friends for specialist information and, above all, for translations. Even so, we are conscious that we may well have some gaps in our coverage.

The work on the "Discourse" was a good illustration that in an historical study of a text the context is all-important, whereas in literature many tell us the text, without its context, is the vital thing. Of the three previous publications of the text those of 1877 and 1935 were lightly annotated; the only one left without comment was that in volume three of our *New American World* of 1979,[24] as that was intended for students to work on texts for themselves. Its special relevance there was

[24] *New American World: A Documentary History of North America to 1612,* ed. D. B. Quinn, with Alison M. Quinn and Susan Hillier (5 vols. New York: Arno Press, 1979), III, 70–123.

that it was included among all the other Elizabethan proposals for American colonization, some of which had not previously appeared in print. Its comparative interest and value could then be estimated as against its alternatives. In fact, none compared with it in scope and scholarship. If Hakluyt was often wrong, he was so because the knowledge of North America available to an Englishman and to Europeans as a whole was still very imperfect. He could do very little more than he achieved in his less than three months' travail. We hope we did him justice, though not giving him more than his due.

THE METAMORPHOSIS OF TRAVELLERS INTO AUTHORS:
THE CASE OF PAUL KANE

I. S. MacLaren

Paul Kane was a Canadian documentary painter of some renown who left little in the way of a written record, though the little he left is very important writing nonetheless. In 1859, *Wanderings of an Artist among the Indians of North America*[1] appeared in London over Kane's name, eleven years after he had returned to Toronto from more than two years of travels with Hudson's Bay Company brigades to the Winnipeg River, the prairies, the Rockies, almost the entire length of the Columbia River, the fledgling Oregon settlement, a smoking Mount St. Helen's, Puget Sound, and Vancouver Island. In this paper I want to place on view the reasons for the need to provide a parallel edition for this text, an edition in which each recto would contain the text of the book, and each facing verso would contain the corresponding field note, where one in Kane's hand exists. It appears that Kane did not write *Wanderings of an Artist,* that is, that his relation to the published narrative does not come within the bounds of what one would regard as the conventional definition of authorship; furthermore, the process by which the nineteenth-century experience of wilderness was encoded in published form needs generally to be brought under scrutiny.

In studying the pre-twentieth-century explorers of and travellers in what is now Canada, one frequently comes to the realization that the narratives published in England over these people's names reflect the taste of the readership of the day as much as they yield insights into the experience of wilderness. The persona of the traveller was made over in the image that his publisher had of what the readership wished. He was washed and shaved, fed and watered, bibbed and tuckered, and

---

[1] Paul Kane, *Wanderings of an Artist among the Indians of North America from Canada to Vancouver's Island and Oregon through the Hudson's Bay Company's Territory and back again* (London: Longman, Brown, Green, Longmans and Roberts, 1859). All references will be to this edition and will appear in parentheses in the text with the designation, *WA*.

readied for presentation in quarto or octavo. Where papers are extant
to permit comparisons, seldom does one find that what was written in
the field or on the seas matches what appears in print. Not often did the
explorer or traveller manage this metamorphosis on his own. The case
of the narrative of Thomas Simpson is an exceptional one. Simpson
was one of two men who between 1836 and 1839 mapped the central
portion of North America's northern coastline. Within ten months of
the completion of his boat surveys with Peter Warren Dease and a crew
of Hudson's Bay Company *engagés*, he had completed a draft manuscript, which was judged nearly fit for the reading public. Edward
Sabine, a career naval officer, explorer, and scientist, who was asked
to prepare it for publication, "found it indeed requiring very little
alteration;—unusually *little*—."[2] But the description "unusually little,"
whatever it may have entailed in the case of Simpson's narrative, does
more than suggest that alteration was common. It also sounds a
cautionary note to scholars, one that echoes back to Bishop John
Douglas's notorious remark regarding the journal of Captain James
Cook's second voyage to the Pacific: "Tho *little* appears to be done by
me," remembered Douglas, "the Journal, if printed as the Captain put
it into my Hands would have been thought too incorrect, & have
disgusted the Reader."[3] But now that books like Paul Carter's *Road to
Botany Bay*, Stephen Greenblatt's *Marvelous Possessions*, Dennis

[2] Letter, Sir Edward Sabine to Sir John Richardson, 9 Feb. 1843; MS
1503/26/2 Richardson-Voss Collection; Scott Polar Research Institute,
Cambridge; quoted by kind permission of Anthony Voss; emphasis added.
Simpson must have prepared his manuscript quickly, because he was dead by
the summer of 1840, within ten months of the men's return to the nearest fur
trade post; see *Narrative of the Discoveries on the North Coast of America;
effected by the Officers of the Hudson's Bay Company during the Years 1836–
39* (London: Richard Bentley, 1843); facs. rpt., 1 vol. in 2 (Toronto:
Canadiana House, 1970). Simpson's gaining an M.A. from the University of
Aberdeen might have had some bearing on his narrative prowess.
[3] John Douglas, "Autobiography" (1776–96), British Library, Egerton MS
2181; quoted by J.C. Beaglehole, ed., *The Journals of Captain James Cook on
His Voyages of Discovery*, 3 vols. in 4. (London: Hakluyt Society, 1955–74),
II, cxliv; emphasis added.

Porter's *Haunted Journeys,* and Mary Louise Pratt's *Imperial Eyes* are offering intensive critical readings of what explorers and travellers apparently wrote and painted, the apparent little that Douglas in 1777 and Sabine in 1843 performed, matters.[4]

To take the slightest example,[5] in the present age of ethno-historical awareness, one is sensitive to a substantive difference between the description in Cook's journal and the description in Douglas's published revision of it of how the Nootka of the west coast of Vancouver Island packed dried sardines into bales. This procedure Cook witnessed during his third voyage, when HMS *Resolution* and *Discovery* anchored at Nootka Sound for a month (30 March–26 April) in 1778. Of the sardines, Cook himself wrote in part as follows: "thus they are kept till wanting and eat very well."[6] "[B]etter stile" is what Douglas considered his contribution to the journals. His revision brings the rhetorical force of litotes to bear on the description: "Thus they are kept till wanted; and they are not a disagreeable article of food."[7] This rhetorical heightening does, in fact, alter Cook's less elevated, north-of-England phrasing, which does not draw attention to itself in the way that the convoluted structure of litotes—the affirmation of something by the negation of its opposite—necessarily does. Simply put, the man who

---

[4] Stephen Greenblatt, *Marvelous Possessions: The Wonder of the New World* (Chicago: University of Chicago Press, 1991); Paul Carter, *The Road to Botany Bay: An Exploration of Landscape and History* (Chicago: University of Chicago Press, 1989); Dennis Porter, *Haunted Journeys: Desire and Transgression in European Travel Writing* (Princeton N.J.: Princeton University Press, 1991); Mary Louise Pratt, *Imperial Eyes: Travel Writing and Transculturation* (New York: Routledge, 1992).

[5] This example and its context receive detailed analysis in MacLaren, "Exploration/Travel Literature and the Evolution of the Author," *International Journal of Canadian Studies/Revue internationale d'études canadiennes* no. 5 (Spring/Printemps 1992), 39–68.

[6] Cook in Beaglehole, ed., *The Journals of Captain James Cook,* III.1, 304.

[7] John Douglas, ed., *A Voyage to the Pacific Ocean. Undertaken, By the Command of His Majesty, for Making Discoveries in the Northern Hemisphere.... Written by Captain James Cook...,* 3 vols. and atlas (London, 1784), II, 280.

finds the fish well kept till wanting and eat very well does not share the linguistic society of the man who finds the fish well kept until wanted, who knows how to use a semicolon, and who judges the fish a not disagreeable article of food. The litotes permits the explorer to suffer the observation at least disinterestedly and perhaps uninterestedly because the circumlocution of the figure rhetorically shields the explorer's civility from the taint of savage custom. The example may seem a slight one, but given that the discourses of imperialism are now groaning under the burden of intense scrutiny, scrutiny often issuing in indictment, it may be that Bishop Douglas's invisible and silent rescue of the explorer from his readers' disgust deserves due attention. It was he, after all, not Cook, who decided that the Nootka were gustatory cannibals, and more than one hundred and seventy-five years passed before that view was overturned by Beaglehole's edition of Cook. Only with its appearance could one readily judge just what "little" Douglas had performed.

In the case of Kane, the published revision of field notes that survive in his hand, far from demonstrating unusually little alteration, evinces a very great deal. Such is the case despite the fact that his book includes what by 1859 had become the familiar disclaimer, the wording of which is instructive, in prefaces to narratives of travel and exploration:

> ...I accordingly kept a diary of my journey, as being the most easy and familiar form in which I could put such information as I might collect. The following pages are the notes of my daily journey, with *little alteration* from the original wording, as I jotted them down in pencil at the time; and although without any claim to public approbation as a literary production, still I trust they will possess not only an interest for the curious, but also an intrinsic value to the historian.... (*WA*, viii; emphasis added)

Moreover, in Kane's case there is the further but complementary, and perhaps pre-eminent, reason for the suitability to this genre of the format of a parallel edition, that is, the fundamental duality that is discernible between the narrative versions accords with the emphatic duality remarked in Kane's art between his field sketches in graphite, watercolour, and oils on the one hand, and his studio oil paintings on the other. But while Kane himself was responsible for both field sketches and studio paintings (although his wife is said to have assisted with the oil paintings, perhaps to a considerable extent[8]), he was not similarly responsible for both narrative versions of his travels. Still, the quintessential duality in each case between field works and the finished, marketable commodity for the civilized, first world cultures of eastern Canada and Britain is analogous. Thus the emphasis in such an edition ought to fall, not on one text, but on the relation between two, in both the narrative and pictorial realms.

The relation between the cases of the words and the images is analogous but not identical; three, not two, stages of the narrative are extant, sufficiently different each to deserve the name of *version* rather than just *text*.[9] The first stage is the field notes in the artist's hand, contained in two breastpocket-sized notebooks suitable for notations while one is *en route*. To the best of anyone's knowledge, they

[8] See M.E. Dignam, "Canadian Women in the Development of Art," in *Women of Canada. Their Life and Work,* comp. by the National Council of Women of Canada for the Minister of Agriculture, ([Ottawa], 1900), 211; also as *Les Femmes du Canada. Leur Vie et leurs Œuvres,* 230. The English-language source is cited by Maria Tippett, *By a Lady: Celebrating Three Centuries of Art by Canadian Women* (Toronto: Viking/Penguin, 1992), 9. The source of Dignam's comment is Sir Daniel Wilson's statement that "[i]n 1853, Mr. Kane married Miss Harriet [Peek] Clench, of Cobourg, a lady who, among other attractions, had a skill with her pencil and brush akin to his own" ("Paul Kane, The Canadian Artist," *The Canadian Journal of Science, Literature, and History,* XIII [1873], 71). Tippett, however, insinuates Clench's participation in Kane's art on no further evidence than this. On the other hand, it is worth noting that the 1849 date of one of Clench's paintings (Fig. 3; and reproduced in Tippett, 10) confirms at least that she was painting in the years between Kane's return from the West and her marriage to him.

[9] I follow the received distinction between *version* and *text,* articulated, for example, in James Thorpe, *Principles of Textual Criticism* (San Marino, Cal.: The Huntington Library, 1972), 185–6.

comprise all the writing Kane did while travelling across North America, including the brief, false start of a trip during the summer of 1845. One of these notebooks contains entries made on a regular, though not always on a daily, basis, from May 1846 until September 1848.[10] There are significant lacunae, however, and discussion will return to them. Although the potential value of these notes was recognized nearly thirty years ago by Kenneth E. Kidd, then of the Royal Ontario Museum, he was unable to do more than browse them in 1954 because his institution had not the wherewithal to purchase at the asking price the 229-item collection of which they formed an inseparable part in the eyes of their owner, Paul Kane III, the Manitoban grandson of the painter.[11] In 1955, he published his view of the significance of the notes,[12] and continued his unsuccessful efforts to

---

[10] Stark Museum of Art, Orange, Texas: 11.85/5.

[11] "Visit to see Paul Kane Sketches in Winnipeg, 1954," Trent University Archives: Kidd, Professor Kenneth; Research Papers Regarding Paul Kane—92-007; quoted by kind permission of the Archivist. Letter, Kenneth E. Kidd to J. Russell Harper, 29 Jan. 1968 (J. Russell Harper Papers, National Archives of Canada, MG 30 D 352, vol. 9, file 10: Correspondence 1964, 1967–9, 1979–80):

> It may interest you to know that I have a set of notes on all of the things I saw in Kane's possession in Winnipeg. He [Paul Kane III] would let me make any notes I wished, except on the field notebook and that I was not allowed to examine at all....
>
> You mention that [Mitchell] Wilder [Director, Amon Carter Museum, Fort Worth, Texas] has, or believes he has, the original manuscript, and that this conflicts with your impression this was destroyed in one of the blitzes. I think there is confusion here. I am pretty sure Wilder does not have a manuscript of Kane's WANDERINGS. What he does have is one (or two?) manuscript notebooks, which from my point of view are much more valuable. I would give ~~anything~~ [inked in above strikeout: a lot] to be able to have a look at them....

In fact, the Stark collection includes both the two-notebook field notes and a four-book draft manuscript. These are discussed below.

[12] "Fortunately, Kane kept a descriptive record of the sketches as he made them, the manuscript of which is still in private possession, and which the

gain access to them after they were sold on 23 September 1957 by Kane to H.J. Lutcher Stark, the Texan collector of western Americana, in a sale that helped to bring about, if not for nearly another two decades, the Canadian Cultural Property Export and Import Act.[13] The contents of this first notebook of field notes were published for the first time only in 1989, in the form of a facsimile version, that is, a clear copy, followed by a "Glossary of Common Words" and a "Guide to People and Places."[14]

Besides a brief narrative of his trip around Lakes Huron and Michigan during the summer of 1845, the second notebook kept by Kane in the field contains a landscape log and a portrait log, narrative descriptions of the scenes that and Indians whom he sketched and

author says he used in writing the book. That the manuscript is still extant is important in itself, for it may contain much that was not considered interesting enough to include in *The Wanderings* but which would be considered important today" (Kidd, "Paul Kane, Painter of Indians," *Bulletin of the Royal Ontario Museum of Archaeology*, no. 23 [May 1955], 12).

[13] Kidd's recollection of events once the collection had changed hands can be summed up in the following: "all my best efforts to see it or to get a copy of it ran up against a stone wall" (Letter, Kenneth E. Kidd to the author, 3 May 1992). Needless to say, the Stark Foundation's policy towards scholars had changed by 1967, in time for J. Russell Harper to undertake his research, and it may fairly be described today as most hospitable (see MacLaren, "Wanderings in Search of Paul Kane's *Wanderings of an Artist*," *Prairie Fire*, 10.3 [Sept. 1989], 28–41).

[14] *The American Art Journal*, XXI.2 (1989), 6–88. These notes were seen by Harper and are referred to as "KJ" and "Kane's Journal" in *Paul Kane's Frontier. Including Wanderings of an Artist among the Indians of North America*, ed., and with biographical introduction and *catalogue raisonné* by J. Russell Harper; published for the Amon Carter Museum, Fort Worth, Texas, and the National Gallery of Canada, Ottawa (Austin, Tex., and London: University of Texas Press; Toronto: University of Toronto Press, 1971); see, in particular, 39, n4. All further references to this edition will appear parenthetically with the name, Harper, in the text, and *catalogue raisonné* will be abbreviated to *cat. rais.*

painted during his transcontinental trip.[15] These are far from complete, given that the entries total 206, while we know that a far greater number of field works are extant. One of these two logs has been published in a greatly altered form, of which more in a moment. Structurally, the two field notebooks together seem like a hybrid of the two titles published by George Catlin in connection with his famous Indian Gallery, apparently seen by Kane in England during his European sojourn. On the one hand, Catlin's two-volume *Letters and Notes*,[16] the fully coloured edition of which bore a slightly different title,[17] provided in fifty-eight letters an account of Catlin's various travels in the American mid-West and prairie-West (Catlin did not cross the Rockies); on the other hand, his *Descriptive Catalogue* provided not only brief notes for the forty-eight tribes represented by the 507 pictures that comprised the Indian Gallery in 1840 and 1841, but also statements by Indian agents and other westerners confirming the authenticity of the illustrations.[18] Perhaps Kane, less confident with words than Catlin, who promoted himself endlessly if not always successfully,[19] took his cue from the American's publications, at least as far as the structure of a prospective book is concerned.[20] To

---

[15] Stark Museum of Art, Orange, Texas: 11.85/4.

[16] *Letters and Notes on the Manners, Customs, and Condition of the North American Indians. by Geo. Catlin. Written during Eight Years' Travel Amongst the Wildest Tribes of Indians in North America. In 1832, 33, 34, 35, 36, 37, 38, and 39.* 2 vols. (London: the Author, 1841).

[17] *The Manners, Customs, and Condition of the North American Indians by George Catlin Written during Eight Years' Travel Amongst the Wildest Tribes of Indians in North America, 1832–39 With Four Hundred Illustrations, carefully engraved from his Original Paintings, and Coloured after Nature In Two Volumes.* 2 vols. (London: the Author, 1841).

[18] *A Descriptive Catalogue of Catlin's Indian Gallery: Containing Portraits, Landscapes, Costumes, &c. and Representations of the Manners and Customs of the North American Indians* (London: the Author, 1840).

[19] See Brian W. Dippie's fine study, *Catlin and His Contemporaries: The Politics of Patronage* (Lincoln and London: University of Nebraska Press, 1990).

[20] The name of George Catlin hangs like a cloud over the study of Kane.

suggest that Kane lacked confidence as an author is *not*, however, to say that he verged on illiteracy; his memorable spellings, for example, nearly always fall within the acceptable limits of canonical orthography, the proof of which is that one very quickly accustoms oneself to them.[21] A not inaccurate description of his style was offered in a memoir by Maude Cassels, the daughter of Kane's patron, George W. Allan:

> He [Kane] says in his admirable preface, "The following pages are the notes of my journey, with little alteration from the original wording as I jotted them in pencil at the time." With less than "a little alteration" they might have gone with

Despite the lack of hard evidence that Kane met him, or that Kane saw Catlin's Indian Gallery at the Egyptian Hall in London when it returned there in 1843 after a tour through other English cities, the notion of Kane as a Canadian Catlin lives on. As far as the writing is concerned, however, it probably deserves to: Kane well knew that comparisons, however adventitious, with Catlin's work would occur, and the American's publications must have been motivations for him when travelling to keep a written account, something one finds no record of his having done when working in Detroit and Alabama or while studying in Europe, and to solicit statements certifying his sketches as authentic (see Harper, *Paul Kane's Frontier*, Appendix 10: letters 7, 9, 11; 328–30).

[21] Kane spells phonetically but within a narrower range of possibilities than anyone who can barely read or write tends to do; that is, he may spell the word *ice* as *ise* but never as *ase* or *oze*. His choices of vowels nearly always make sense if one is prepared to accept that the sound of an *e*, for example, as it appears in another word in the language is a possible spelling for him. Nor do Kane's writings show consistent signs of dialect. "Thare" as in "I came to rite thare portraits" might sound Irish, but only if one hears it as "thar" (or is "thar" the rendering one inclines to because of the stereotypical accent associated with the mountain man of the American frontier?); if one hears it as the sound made by the combination of *a*, *r*, and *e* in words like bare, rare, hare, mare, dare, and so on, it is no surprise; indeed, the same sound made by the combination of *e*, *i*, and *r* is very uncommon in English. I am grateful for comments on Kane's spelling from John Hogan, Professor of Linguistics, University of Alberta.

more of a swing, though something, I suppose had to be
done about about the original spelling, as Kane in a hurry
spelt like a little child, or an 18th century gentleman.[22]

The second stage of the narrative may never have existed, and has not
come to light. This is the journal stage in the four-part model that
appears generally appropriate for the genre of the exploration and travel
narrative. Although somewhat confusing (because journal often appears
as a synonym for diary and field notes), this stage is meant to refer to
the traveller's retrospective writing up of his travels upon completion
of them, or an important stage of them. Elsewhere, I have outlined my
reasons for according this a stage of its own in the model.[23]

The third stage is the draft manuscript, not in Kane's hand except
in the case of some interlineations and most of the marginal numerical
references to sketches. The manuscript is contained in four hardback
books, of which only the fourth has been published; that publication is
a highly edited and silently corrected version, forming the second
appendix of Harper's impressive and mammoth study, *Paul Kane's
Frontier* (Harper, 315–17). Because the first and the fourth of these
manuscript books bear almost identical titles, one might think they
represent what Harper refers to when he states that, "[t]wo manuscript
versions of *Wanderings of an Artist,* also in the Stark Foundation
collections, were used by the editor in preparing the present text"
(Harper, [i]). They do not, however, amount to two discrete or completed versions.[24] But because Harper also had studied the two small

[22] Maude Cassels, "Paul Kane," typescript dated March 1932, Department of
Ethnology, Royal Ontario Museum, p. 16; quoted by kind permission of
Kenneth R. Lister, Curatorial Assistant, Department of Ethnology.

[23] MacLaren, "Exploration/Travel Literature and the Evolution of the Author";
see also MacLaren, "Samuel Hearne's Accounts of the Massacre at Bloody
Fall, 17 July 1771," *Ariel: A Review of International English Literature,* 22.1
(Jan. 1991), 25–51.

[24] Stark Museum of Art, Orange, Texas. The first three books are 11.85/2 (A),
11.85/2 (B), and 11.85/2 (C). They bear the title "Pictorial Sketches with
Historical Notices taken during two journeys across the American Continent to

field notebooks, it is probable that by "[t]wo manuscript versions" he meant the two-notebook field notes as one, and the four books of the draft manuscript as the other. Yet, his study's first two appendices in fact confuse the two versions. Working from the principle that the appendices ought to include only information not contained in the text of the first edition of *Wanderings of an Artist,* he edits liberally. In the case of Appendix 1, which he titles "Paul Kane's Landscape Log, Kept on His 1846–48 Journey" (Harper, 313–15), his copy-text was the second notebook of field notes. In the case of Appendix 2, titled "Paul Kane's Portrait Log, Kept on His 1846–48 Journey" (Harper, 315–17), the copy-text was the fourth book of the draft manuscript, which was neither kept on the journey nor written in Kane's hand. Like the fourth book of the draft manuscript, this appendix extends only to an eighty-eighth entry but Kane's own portrait log, kept in the second notebook during the journey, has ninety-seven entries and those ninety-seven do not comprise all the eighty-eight in the draft manuscript. The reason for this confusion remains unclear; Harper may not have sorted out in his own mind just how the various manuscripts related to one another, and did not have the benefit of an examination of them except in photographic form, illness having forced him to cancel his one planned trip to Texas during the course of his research.[25] In any case, evidence

the Columbia River and North West Coast of the Pacific in the years 1845, 1846, 1847 & 1848 by Paul Kane." The fourth is 11.85/3. It bears the similar but not quite identical title, "Pictorial Sketches with Historical notices taken during two journeys across the Continent of America to the Columbia River & North West coast of the Pacific in the years 1845 1846–1847 & 1848 by Paul Kane." The considerable overlap between 11.85/2 (A) and (B) suggests that the entire manuscript was begun again shortly after the second distinguishable handwriting begins. For a description of the relation of these manuscript books to one another and to the corresponding chapter of *Wanderings of an Artist,* see MacLaren, "Notes Towards a Reconsideration of Paul Kane's Art and Prose," *Canadian Literature,* nos. 113–114 (Summer/Fall 1987), 179–205; esp. 193–4.

[25] A very brief trip to Texas was planned for late November 1969, but ill health prevented Harper's making it. (See J. Russell Harper Papers, National Archives of Canada, MG 30 D 352, vol. 10: Correspondence 1969–1983.) Francess G. Halpenny, then senior editor at the University of Toronto Press,

forces one to reject the claim made in the note to Appendix 1 and repeated for Appendix 2, that "[t]he wording and spelling of Kane's original are followed" (Harper, 313); they are not for the first appendix, nor are they for the second, where the spelling is someone else's to begin with.

A digression is required to discuss this problem in Harper's work. Perhaps the burden of making Kane the father of art in English-speaking Canada at the time of the Canadian centennial and of the centennial (1971) of Kane's death exerted a familiar claim to perform a *little* alteration in what otherwise appears rather ragged writing, the product of a rough and ready traveller, not quite appropriate as a figure of national history, who, in any event, apparently revised all those notes and produced a famous book from them. Clearly, similar efforts had been made in Kane's lifetime to present him as the author of his book. And they were still ongoing in 1954 when Kenneth Kidd was invited by Paul Kane III to view his collection in Winnipeg: the grandson, still seeking a considerable sum for the collection and perhaps fearing the diminishment of its value if Kane's own unsophisti-cated writings became known, would not permit the two field notebooks to be examined.[26] From this it may be seen that Harper was not the

who worked very closely with Harper on his book, has confirmed verbally that he was unable to visit the collection. The photographs from which Harper produced transcriptions are in the Harper Papers, National Archives of Canada, MG 30 D 352, vol. 12, 12-1 to 12-5, 12-8 to 12-13, and vol. 13, 13-1 to 13-8. In Harper's typed transcriptions of both the field notebooks and the draft manuscripts, which comprise vol. 12, 12-6 and 12-7, it appears that he was supplied with no distinctions among the items received; simply, rolls of developed film were sent to him, and the titles for and pagination of his transcriptions do not have them sorted out accurately.

[26] Although Paul Kane III had gone out of his way to lambaste John W. Garvin and Lawrence J. Burpee for inaccuracies in introducing Kane for the first Canadian edition of *Wanderings of an Artist* (Toronto: The Radisson Society, 1925), and although in "A Criticism" (c.1925) of that edition he draws and quarters Burpee for failing to appreciate Kane's sketches, he is himself very careful to keep hidden what must have been his own presentiments about the distant relation between his grandfather and the authorship of *Wanderings*. In

first to guard Kane's image. But it is important that the possible reasons raised not go misunderstood, especially as Harper's was ground-breaking, and, in terms of its art history, exceedingly thorough work. The prospect of an enormously large book by Canadian art historical standards was in itself formidable: one reviewer noted that *Paul Kane's Frontier* was "believe it or not the first complete study and catalogue of a Canadian artist to appear, ever."[27]

Coincidental with the book's publication were a similarly extensive tour of 171 of Kane's works to six cities across the continent and the international border, as well as a CBC documentary—even a seven-cent stamp was issued to honour the centenary of the artist's death. These factors may have conspired to amplify the stature of the subject. Certainly, the market on both sides of the border proved very interested in the product. In the case of Canada, on 29 May 1971, when cultural nationalism and literary merit put Robertson Davies' *Fifth Business* at the top of national bestsellers of fiction, a rare appearance was made on the list of top ten bestsellers of non-fiction by an academic title: the sales of *Paul Kane's Frontier* were rivalling those of *The National Dream*, by Pierre Berton, no stranger to such lists, and of famous titles like *The Greening of America, Future Shock,* and *White Niggers of America.*[28]

"A Criticism," six foolscap pages of single-spaced expressions of outrage, Kane III words the significant passage so that *Wanderings* was not written by, but, rather, "published in London in 1859 by Paul Kane, the Canadian artist. The original publication," the grandson deftly argues in the manner of the lawyer he was, "*embodied* Kane's daily journal or diary" ("Wanderings of an Artist... 1925... A Criticism By Paul Kane — [A Grandson]," photocopy in the Harper Papers, National Gallery of Canada, MG 30 D 352, vol. 13, 13-13, 1; all attempts at locating the original have been unsuccessful; a portion of "A Criticism" appeared in *The Canadian Bookman* 8[1926], 245-55. I am grateful to Robert Stacey for bringing the abridged published source of this response to my attention).

[27] David Silcox, The Globe Magazine, 22 May 1971, 15.

[28] "National Bestsellers," Toronto Daily Star, 29 May 1971; copy in National Archives of Canada, Harper Papers, MG 30 D 352, vol. 43, file 23: Reviews 1971.

The august and well received multi-volume *Journals of the Lewis & Clark Expedition* began its project at the conclusion of the American bicentennial celebrations. Five years later (ten years ago), the first volume appeared with the announcement that "[t]he journals of the two Captains and of four enlisted men are American treasures."[29] Are they? Or is the scale of the project such that they cannot help but be? That external pressures exert themselves on editorial projects is no less true today than it was three decades or much longer ago. At least three such pressures are notable now. One comes in the form of the remarkably increasing interest in the narratives of travel and exploration, which such events as the Columbus quincentenary have spawned, thereby almost automatically calling for a new edition of *Wanderings of an Artist* and other narratives of New World travel that are out of print. Another, complementary to it, is post-colonialism's overweening urge within academic discourse to discount or disparage the colonial past as the product of the reprehensible discourse of imperialism.[30] And a third, again related, is contemporary critical attitudes: by emphasising Kane's field work in both narrative and art, a convincing argument can be made that on his own he was not the mouthpiece of racist imperialism that his book makes him out to be in the current climate of Columbian revisionism. Kane can be largely exempted from charges by, and even recuperated rather fortuitously in the name of, white majoritarian Canada's guilt-ridden political correctness, different in type but not in degree from the equally widespread and well-meaning political correctness of cultural nationalism in the Canada of the late 1960s and early 1970s. That is, like Bishop Douglas, the editor of Kane's own writings could furnish a narrative that did not disgust its contemporary reader.

In the four books of this third stage, the draft manuscript, it appears that two other hands than Kane's are at work. There is a

[29] Gary E. Moulton, "Preface," *Atlas of the Lewis & Clark Expedition*, vol. 1 of *The Journals of the Lewis and Clark Expedition*, ed. by Gary E. Moulton (Lincoln and London: University of Nebraska Press, 1983), [vii].

[30] See Heather Dawkins, "Paul Kane and the Eye of Power: Racism in Canadian Art History," *Vanguard*, vol. 15, no. 4 (Sept. 1986), 24–7.

possibility that one of them, responsible for some writing in the first and all of it in the second, third, and fourth books, is that of Harriet Peek Clench Kane (1823–1892; Fig. 2), whom Kane married in 1853, and whom he had probably known since 1834, when he lived in Cobourg, where he perhaps worked for her father's cabinet making business as a decorative furniture painter; if he did, he also would have boarded at the Clench house (Harper, 10–11). This possibility is founded on a resemblance in handwriting. It is known that Harriet Peek Clench wrote the catalogue for Kane's exhibition of sketches in November 1848, a month after his return to Toronto. Although the capital letters in this list are somewhat stylized for the occasion, the handwriting in normal words such as "great," "from," and "village" resembles the handwriting of the main portion of the draft manuscript.[31] And the same handwriting in the draft manuscript accords with a letter written by Harriet to her mother in 1884, much later in life.[32] However, conclusive comparisons of the hands are not possible.

From the editorial point of view, this draft manuscript is not reliable except for studying the evolution of the narrative from Kane's own field notes to the published form of the narrative. If one envisages the evolution of Kane's book as a migration eastward, from the field notes made in the wilderness West to the book published in the imperial centre of London, then one can plot the draft manuscript mid-way along that path, as a ten-year, four-book layover in Toronto. During

[31] Compare, for example, the word "from" in the draft manuscript, 11.85/2 (B), [f.22r], line 14, with the same word in the catalogue, under the title for items 18, 32, and 54; the word "great" in the draft manuscript, 11.85/2 (B), [f.18r], line 22, with the same word in the catalogue, item 16; and the word "village" in the draft manuscript, 11.85/3, p. 43, line 9, with the same word in the catalogue, under the title for item 225. ("Catalogue of Sketches of Indians and Indian Chiefs, Landscapes, Dances, Costumes, &c. &c. By Paul Kane. Toronto, November, 1848." Royal Ontario Museum, Department of Ethnology. The attribution of the handwriting in this catalogue to Clench is that of Kenneth R. Lister, Curatorial Assistant, Department of Ethnology, Royal Ontario Museum, who bases it on the signature on her will.)

[32] Letter, Harriet Peek Clench Kane to Mrs. F.S. Clench, 3 Oct. 1884; Lowe Family fonds, National Archives of Canada, MG 30 D 35.

this intermediate period, the narrative grows another version, but hardly with Harriet Clench's assistance only, for much of the new information in the draft manuscript could have been told to her only by Kane or someone else who had travelled west, and in some cases by someone in possession of more detailed information about the route and about aboriginal people than, judging by his own writings, the wandering artist himself possessed. Here, however, one leaves relatively substantiable fact and embarks on speculation.

Who are the chief possible contributors to the draft manuscript? One candidate is Sir Daniel Wilson, who arrived in Toronto in 1854 as the university's most distinguished professor and whose interest in ethnography was unmatched in the city. Wilson soon befriended Kane and later used two of his sketches as frontispieces for his own, two-volume book, *Prehistoric Man,* in which he occasionally identifies Kane as an ethnographic authority (because an eyewitness) and quotes from *Wanderings of an Artist.*[33] As well, he wrote Kane's obituary, which is the source of the information that Harriet possessed as much skill as Paul with pencil and brush. Unfortunately, Wilson insisted that upon his death his papers be burned, so the prosecution of that candidacy is not hopeful.[34] Aspects of Kane's narrative do, however, offer tantalizing echoes of Wilson's own view. One, so often quoted when Kane's book is described, pertains to the view of the certain disappearance of native peoples. This view was widespread, of course, and Kane's reiteration is nothing unique:

> I had been accustomed to see hundreds of Indians about my native village, then Little York, muddy and dirty, just

---

[33] Sir Daniel Wilson, *Prehistoric Man: Researches into the Origin of Civilisation in the Old and New World,* 2 vols., Cambridge and London: Macmillan, 1862. In his preface, Wilson identifies Kane as the author of *Wanderings,* and goes on to thank him for "sketches made during his travels, as well as for information derived from recollections of the incidents and observations of a highly-privileged sojourner among the Indian tribes of the Hudson's Bay territory" (I, xv).

[34] Carl Berger, "Sir Daniel Wilson," *DCB,* XII, 1113.

struggling into existence, now the City of Toronto, bursting
forth in all its energy and commercial strength. But the face
of the red man is now no longer seen. All traces of his
footsteps are fast being obliterated from his once favourite
haunts, and those who would see the aborigines of this
country in their original state, or seek to study their native
manners and customs, must travel far through the pathless
forest to find them. (*WA*, vii)

Kane's field notes offer no early version for this view or even for the
echo, repeated in this passage, of Catlin's title, *Manners and Customs*,
but what suggests Wilson's hand in such a conventional utterance is
that, concerned generally with the topic of the extinction of races
throughout history, he discoursed on it in 1856 in *The Canadian
Journal*, the publication of the Canadian Institute, before which some
preliminary chapters of Kane's book were read. Although Wilson
considered absorption more accurate than extinction as a description of
the evolution of race, his prelusive statement demonstrates his keen
awareness of the level of public interest in the subject during the mid-
nineteenth century:

Among the many difficult problems which the thoughtful
observer has to encounter, in an attempt to harmonise the
actual with his ideal of the world as the great theatre of the
human race, none assumes a more intricate and inexplicable
aspect than the displacement and extinction of races, such as
the Anglo-Saxon has witnessed on this continent for upwards
of two centuries. In all ages history discloses to us unmis-
takeable evidence, not only of the distinctions which civilization produces, but of the fundamental differences whereby a
few highly favoured races have outsped all others; triumph-
ing in the onward progress of the nations, not less by an
innate constitutional superiority, than by an acquired civilization, or by local advantages. And if we are still troubled with
the perplexities of this dark riddle, whereby the Colonists of
the new world only advance by the retrogression of the Red

> Man, and tread, in our western progress, on the graves of
> nations, it may not be without its interest to note some
> unmistakeable evidences of this process of displacement and
> extinction, accompanying the progress of the human race
> from the very dawn of history.[35]

Moreover, Wilson's interest in understanding the precedents for
absorption must have made him sympathetic to Kane's effort to
document natives prior to their certain absorption, if not prior to all
contact with white civilization, "which brings for him only vice,
famine, and disease, in its train."[36]

Another possible contributor to the manuscript is Henry Youle
Hind, who edited *The Canadian Journal,* in which excerpts from
Wanderings of an Artist were printed in the early 1850s after being
read as papers to the Canadian Institute (read by whom is unclear:
Wilson was also much involved in the institute and its journal). A year
after Kane's *Wanderings* appeared, Longman, Green, Longman and
Roberts also published Hind's account of western travel and survey.[37]

Another candidate seems to be Sir John Henry Lefroy, the British
scientist and colonial administrator who had travelled with Hudson's
Bay Company brigades west in 1843 and as far north as Fort Good
Hope, on the lower Mackenzie River. He wrote Kane a letter of
introduction to gain him access to Sir George Simpson, governor of the
Hudson's Bay Company (Harper, 16–17), he served as president of the
Canadian Institute in the early 1850s, and he is said to have helped
Kane gain audiences with publishers once the Canadian arrived in
London in late 1858, perhaps with his four hardback books of the draft

---

[35] Daniel Wilson, "Displacement and Extinction Among the Primeval Races of
Man," *The Canadian Journal of Industry, Science, and Art,* n.s., vol. 1, no.
1 (Jan. 1856), 4.

[36] Wilson, "Displacement and Extinction," 12.

[37] *Narrative of the Canadian Red River Exploring Expedition of 1857 and of the
Assiniboine and Saskatchewan Exploring Expedition of 1858,* 2 vols. (London:
Longman, Green, Longman and Roberts, 1860).

manuscript under his arm.[38] Apparently Kane painted Lefroy in a fanciful winter travelling scene (although the elongated and slender demeanour of the figure and the brightness of the colours used do not remind one of Kane's style).[39] As a final speculation, one must consider that the publication date of *Wanderings of an Artist,* March of 1859, makes reasonable an involvement on the part of the Hudson's Bay Company itself; aware that its exclusive charter to trade in more than one-quarter of the entire continent was to expire in 1859, Simpson or members of his board might well have taken an interest in the publication of Kane's book, the first about the entire West to appear over the name of a non-fur-trader, and, therefore, capable of being regarded as an objective account.[40]

This last speculation, however, pertains rather to the fourth-stage narrative, the published book itself. Before I turn to that discussion, a more substantial factor requires consideration. Offered unsolicited in interviews and correspondence with descendants both of Kane and of Harriet Peek Clench Kane was the family story that Harriet wrote her husband's book. Usually, scholars must be very careful with such evidence (although, if it issues from oral cultures, we seem prepared these days to accept it with alacrity). In this case, before samples of handwriting became available for comparison, both Mary Evelyn Kane, the widow of Paul Kane III, and her daughter, and Jessie Lowe, the great niece of Harriet and an avid and accomplished genealogist of the Clench, Cory, and Armour families, related this story; they expressed surprise that it was not better known, and wondered why it much mattered.[41] They adduced Kane's apparent snow blindness as the need

---

[38] Carol M. Whitfield and Richard A. Jarrell, "Sir John Henry Lefroy," *DCB,* XI, 508–10.

[39] Paul Kane, *The Surveyor: Portrait of Captain John Henry Lefroy.* c.1855 oil on canvas. 56.2 × 76.5 cm. Glenbow-Alberta Institute 55.31.3; not mentioned in Harper, *cat. rais.*

[40] See MacLaren, "Creating Travel Literature: The Case of Paul Kane," *Papers of the Bibliographical Society of Canada,* 27 (1988), 80–95; esp. 90–2.

[41] Interview with Mary Evelyn Kane, 4 Aug. 1989; interview with Jessie Lowe, 9 Feb. 1992.

for this assistance, however. On the other hand, their view of Harriet made her a strong possibility, especially as it is known, from her writing of the catalogue for the November 1848 exhibition of sketches, that she and Kane were working together very soon after his return from the West in October of that year. Photos of them individually are instructive. One shows a bohemian strain in Kane (Fig. 1) and, as if to encourage that interpretation of his character, bears the caption in what appears to be Kane's hand, "The Porcupine." By contrast, Harriet was genteel (Fig. 2).[42]

In the late 1830s and 1840s, Cobourg, at about 3,000 inhabitants the same size as York (after 1834, Toronto), was as fine an address as any in Canada West, better than Susanna Moodie's Belleville of the late 1830s and beyond, and as good as anything Toronto might boast of. It was in Cobourg that Egerton Ryerson had presided over the establishment in 1836 and the growth of the Upper Canada Academy, which, as Victoria College, began conferring degrees in 1842; it did so there for another five decades before the college moved to Toronto in 1892, the year of Harriet Clench's death. Culturally, architecturally, and socially, Cobourg was a force to contend with in the decades when Harriet Clench was reared, educated, and polished. If that was not enough, her Loyalist stock would have helped define her acculturation. Family history also suggests that a deformity in the shape of the right side of her mouth presented problems for her socially, ones that artistic achievements could overcome.

Kane certainly seems to have been a bohemian at heart; had he lived at the turn of the century, one surmises that Bliss Càrman and Richard Hovey's initiation of the vogue of vagabondia might have

---

[42] Three details suggest an unconfirmed date of c.1850 for this photograph: the youthful appearance of Harriet relative to other photographs of her; the Zouave jacket worn by her, a style fashionable in the 1850s; and the place—Cobourg —where, it may be inferred from a stamp on the verso, the photograph was taken by E. Stanton. Because other photographs of her at an evidently older age bear the stamps of photographers in Toronto, it seems likely that this dates the photo to a time prior to Harriet's marriage and permanent move to Toronto, that is, prior to 1853.

found in him an eager devotee. Occasional appearances — only in the field notes — of a wry sense of humour, and his reputation for not being socially tactful or grateful (Harper, 39) perhaps confirm this view. As a portrait painter, in Detroit and Mobile, then as a sometime student of art in Italy, and finally as a transcontinental wilderness traveller, he must have seen several sides of life during the period from ages 26 (1836) to 38 (1848), sides that perhaps diverged from the strict moral tone of Upper Canada in the first half of the nineteenth century.[43] As well, if studies in Europe did not enthral him, his contact with native societies intrigued and impressed him forcefully; upon his return to Toronto in 1848, despite a debt to Sir George Simpson amounting to twelve oil paintings, Kane made every effort to head west again as early as 1849, and did so, reaching Fort Garry before being fired for failing to live up to his claim as a competent guide (Harper, 30–2). In short, a reading of Kane's field notes presents a character quite distinct from the English sporting gentleman who narrates *Wanderings of an Artist,* the sort of man who might have found a place among the assembled in Clench's *Country Tavern near Cobourg* (Fig. 3).

This upgrading of social class by means of the narrator's characterization marks one of the widest distinctions between the field notes and the draft manuscript. In the latter, which also directs more light more often on the person of Kane, the narrator/traveller/persona is not the same man. Not only diction but the introduction of compound sentence structures that lay beyond the grasp of Kane's own pen effect the change. For example, in early July 1846, Kane wrote in what for him is some detail about four different people whom he encountered in succession when endeavouring to sketch a Saulteaux near the mouth of the Red River. The draft manuscript restructures the scene, adds details, presents the figure of Kane more prominently, and forms the

---

[43] See William H. Westfall, *Two Worlds: The Protestant Culture of Nineteenth-Century Ontario* (Kingston and Montréal: McGill-Queen's University Press, 1989); and Mary Lu MacDonald, *Literature and Society in the Canadas 1817–1850* (Lewiston, N.Y., Queenston, Ont., Lampeter, Penn.: Edwin Mellen Press, 1992).

whole into sentences. The first version is Kane's own. It remains faithful to his spelling and the line breaks in his small, breastpocket-sized notebook:

> they Indans crowded about
> the boat and wanted to
> know what we wanted
> I tould them that I
> came to rite thare po
> =rtraits (they way they
> express them selfs) a man
> stept up and toald me to
> take him he was as natur
> made him (he was nacad
>) I declined the honner
> I wanted take a young wom
> =an but she sade that she
> could not dress her self
> as she had lost sum
> of her frinds I got a
> young Gerl to set in
> her Native costume
> her Mother wanted
> know if she would
> not com to sum har
> =m by it her name was
> the constant scie
> an Indan here offer=
> =ed to give us a fare
> wind for 3 dayes for
> a pound of tobackeo[44]

It is complemented by a brief entry in his field portrait log:

[44] Stark Museum of Art, Orange, Texas: 11.85/5, [29–30].

No 5
Caw-ce-ca.ce che-cock
A Soto the constant
skey her mother
wanted to know if
it would hurt her
to sit for her pic
ture.[45]

The number at the head of the entry corresponds with that on a particular sketch, which can therefore be accurately identified, and might take the name, "Caw-ce-ca.ce che-cock: the constant scie/Skey"; however, because it occurs on the right hand side of a page that contains another sketch, it is known simply as "Two Indian Portraits" (Fig. 4). On that sketch as well, an erroneous identification, not in Kane's hand, reads: "Indians of same tribe from Lake Superior."
    The second book of the draft manuscript offers an account of this scene in the context of the narrative of daily events, while the fourth provides an entry in the draft of the portrait log. They are, respectively, as follows (again, with the original line breaks retained):

The Indians crowded round the boat on our
arrival, enquiring what we wanted =
Our man who interpreted for us told them
that I had come to "write their likenesses", this
being their mode of expression — One of them entirely
~~without~~ naked, stepped up telling me to write
his likeness, as he was just as the great spirit
made him — I declined ~~doing as he wished~~ acceding
    to his request —
A young woman whom I wanted to sketch, refused,
~~on the~~ saying she had just lost some of her
relations and could not dress herself suitably
for such an occasion — their mourning dress

[45] Stark Museum of Art, Orange, Texas: 11.85/4, [51–2].

  always consisting of their oldest and worst
  clothes, as the custom of the tribe forbids any
  finery being worn for several months after the
  death of a near relation — I succeeded however
  in inducing a young girl to sit to me in
  ~~Her native Soto~~ the costume of the tribe — her mother
  wanted to know if any harm would result
  from it, to her life ~~her~~ On my ~~assuring~~ telling her that
  she might perhaps live the longer, she readily
  consented to her doing so = this ~~is a~~ superstition
  pervadin~~ges~~ almost every tribe ~~of~~ I have met
  with on the continent — After finishing my
  sketch, which they all looked at with astonish-
  ment, a ~~one of their~~ "Medicine men" [*sic*] stepped up
  and told us that he would give us three days [*sic*]
  fair wind for a pound of tobacco, a demand so
  enormous for so small a supply of wind that we immediately
    declined the bargain
  whereupon he unhesitatingly reduced his price
  offering a greater quantity of wind for a smaller
  ~~weight~~ amount of tobacco till at length having reduced
  his price to a small plug ~~of tobacco~~ for six
  days ~~wind~~ we closed the bargain—[46]

In the draft manuscript of the portrait log, the girl's name appears
again, newly spelled, but more attention is focused on the other girl,
who refuses to be painted, and the order is switched round:

  5.
  Cawkeekaikee~~y eekoke~~koke (the constant sky) a Soto girl —
  her mother for some time refused to allow me to
  take her likeness — on the old grounds that it might
  shorten her days — this prejudice I had to combat
  as I had repeatedly done before, and as often

---

[46] Stark Museum of Art, Orange, Texas: 11.85/2 (B), 48r, 49r, 50r.

since — she at length acceded to my request — I
saw at this camp of Indians a rather good looking girl
   whom I tried to
persuade to wash the grease & dirt from
her face and sit to me, with this however
the customs of her tribe forbad her acquiescence
as she was then in mourning for the loss of a
relative and not allowed to cleanse her person
or apparel for a year — she had not
then washed herself for 3 months — altho her
thin apparel was disgustingly filthy she showed
me a ~~ward~~ [wardrobe?] number of handsome
   Indian female dresses —[47]

Did Harriet assemble these two scenes in the draft manuscript, both of which establish more formal relations between Kane and the four individuals? The colloquialism, "rite their portraits," unfortunately disappears, replaced by the colourless and merely conventional "write their likenesses," and so the new appositive, "this being their mode of expression," lacks the interest that Kane's parenthesis, "(the way they express themselfs)," lent his original phrasing. And that authority is entirely vitiated in the draft portrait log, where it becomes merely "take her likeness." Similarly, the field note's "he was as natur made him (he was nacad)" is altered and yields the impression that the man appears deficient rather than natural—"entirely naked"—and registers him in the stereotypical fashion by which travel narratives simultaneously acknowledged and patronized the spiritual dimension of native cultures—"as the great spirit made him." The characteristic dry humour, in the remark "I declined the honner," also disappears, replaced once again by conventional remarks. Next, whereas the Kane of the field note is silent, into the mouth of Kane's persona in the draft manuscript is placed the reasoning by which he wins the consent of the girl who goes unnamed until the draft of the portrait log. And note that

[47] Stark Museum of Art, Orange, Texas: 11.85/3, [66]–67.

he wins with artifice—the fillip that her acquiescence might lengthen her life; in this way he preys on the native "superstition" ("prejudice" in the entry for the draft portrait log) of the powers of his artistry, even while he scorns it. The fact that every tribe he meets betrays this quality then takes that quality out of context and projects it onto the entire continent's native people so that the specificity of the occasion is lost. Finally, the man who offers fair winds for tobacco makes his first appearance as a "'Medicine man'" only in the draft manuscript. His powers as a medicine man are implicitly set against the painter's and they lose. In the draft manuscript, the man is humiliated, whereas in the field note the event has no conclusion, the only implication perhaps being that Kane was amused by the offer of fair sailing.

These are some of the substantive stylistic alterations, but they also involve substantive changes in content. On the credit side perhaps, the draft manuscript offers the amplification of Kane's own rather opaque account of the other girl's reason for refusing to be painted, as well as the information that the medicine man was beaten down in price until there was nothing left of his offer, which may have been a charade (although one cannot judge as much with certainty because that inference is drawn from the adverb, "unhesitatingly," which changes to "hesitatingly" by the time of the book's publication.) Also added are the explanation of the period of mourning and the description of the woman's grease, dirt, and "disgustingly filthy" "apparel": did these offend Kane's wife more than Kane himself? Certainly the description begins to sound stereotypical in a way that it does not in Kane's briefer field note, and the content begins to contend with the tone; for example, in the draft manuscript alone, this filthy woman nevertheless turns a dainty syntactical demurral: "with this [request] however the customs of her tribe forbad her acquiescence." The nice phrasing flatters Kane's writerly competence and patronizes, if it does not mock, the woman.

Although further textual and literary interpretation is possible, these substantive variants between field notes and draft manuscripts indicate that once other writers begin to contribute to the narrative it begins to grow in ways that are not always consonant with one another. Like Nathaniel Hawthorne's wife, who was rendering a similar service to her husband's manuscripts in the same decade,[48] Harriet seems to have known how to refine both wording and characterization to conform to the tastes of the day, but her or someone else's metamorphosis of Kane's persona leaves him an odd figure, not permitted to be as fascinated with native lifeways as he so obviously was. In short, the painter of Indians seems to despise them. Whereas the reader finds Bishop Douglas's litotes shielding Cook from the baled sardines, one must contend in the draft manuscript (and later, in the book) with both revulsion at natives and eagerness to meet, paint, and collect artifacts from them.[49]

The fourth stage of this narrative is the famous book, *Wanderings of an Artist among the Indians of North America*. It need not be described at length, but a few matters deserve attention in the light of a textual discussion. One is that no evidence survives to suggest that Kane responded other than affirmatively to the narrative metamorphosis taking place over his name. Another is that by all accounts the book proved a success for Longman, and, to the extent that it sold well, owed something to the conventional representation of the sophisticated

---

[48] *The English Notebooks of Nathaniel Hawthorne*, ed. by Randall Stewart (New York: Yale University Press, 1941), ix–xxi; cited by Thorpe, *Principles of Textual Criticism*, 19.

[49] Harper did not push his enquiry so far, but it should be noted that he was aware of the need for subsequent research. At an early point in his own research, he jotted down points for discussion that he thought his introduction ought to broach. The last of them are these: "Two Mss revisions - wife's hand? How closely has he followed original journal? ~~embellishment~~? - Various editions - Reviews[;] Imitation of Catlin's book" (National Archives of Canada, Harper Papers, MG 30 D 352, vol. 10, file 1: Correspondence 1969–1971). One simply cannot read the three versions of this narrative of impressive adventure and geographical comprehensiveness without wondering about Kane's role as its author. Harper struck out the word "embellishment" and probably ran into a dead end with the query, "wife's hand." He turned his almost infinite attention to forming a *catalogue raisonné*, produced an annotated edition of the first edition of *Wanderings of an Artist*, and was working — feverishly is not too strong a description — on *A People's Art*, an equally successful book, even before *Paul Kane's Frontier* had appeared.

artist-traveller-sportsman-gentleman. The evolution of Kane from
unpublished wanderer into published artist qualified him in a way that
his own writings definitely could not have, as one deserving of the
carte blanche he received from the Hudson's Bay Company, which
usually reserved place only for passengers of relatively high social
standing, or emissaries of government or religion. In short, the man,
if he were to become published, had to be seen to deserve such
hospitable passage through what amounted to the private syndicate, or,
as the book's subtitle puts it, the "territory," of the Hudson's Bay
Company. And could an English publishing house afford to market the
narrative of an eccentric traveller when the eccentricity was not one of
genius but of class? One must recall how competitive the market for
travel narratives was in the mid-nineteenth century. As Royal Gettman's study of the Bentley firm indicates, few of them sold in
sufficient numbers to realize their publisher a profit:

> although the nineteenth-century Briton was an inveterate
> traveller and although he was much given to writing of his
> travels—Richard Bentley and Son published 367 such
> books—there may have been more than a grain of truth in
> Byron's lines[, written early on in the century, in 1821]:
> [I won't describe; description is my forte,]
>   But every fool describes in these bright days
> His wond'rous journey to some foreign court,
>   And spawns his quarto, and demands your praise—
> Death to his publisher, to him 'tis sport....[50]

Kane and his helpers spawned a modest octavo, with engravings,
of only modest merit, and made Longman money: within three months

---

[50] Royal A. Gettman, *A Victorian Publisher: A Study of the Bentley Papers*
(Cambridge: Cambridge University Press, 1960), 134. I am grateful to Ian
Willison for bringing Gettman's study to my attention. The supplementary line
from *Don Juan* is quoted from *Don Juan* (1821) Canto V, 412; in *Lord Byron:
The Complete Poetical Works,* ed. by Jerome J. McGann, 6 vols. (Oxford:
Clarendon, 1986), V, 257.

of the book's appearance, 747 of the 1000 copies printed had been sold. But before a single copy appeared, much more revising occurred. Kane's narrative had been gentrified before he sailed to England, but the manuscript still lacked chapter and often paragraph divisions, for example. Harper is perfectly right to nominate the draft manuscript an "early version" and to infer that a later one, from which the published text was set, probably was destroyed along with so many of the papers of Longman in the London blitz (Harper, 40). By 17 March 1859, when a copy of *Wanderings* was registered by the publisher at Stationers' Hall, more than one editor's services apparently had been engaged, for whereas Kane received six complementary copies of the book, the Longman Divide Ledger indicates that "editors" received eighteen copies.[51] Moreover, some of the content was still lacking.

One example may serve for a great many, and the illustrations may be viewed analogously. The ninety-second entry in Kane's field landscape log reads as follows: "92. the game of Alcolach plaid for 2 Horses."[52] The corresponding sketch is "The game of Al-kol-lock, Columbia River" (Fig. 5), made by Kane at Fort Colville, on the Columbia River, just inside the American border, in late August or early September, 1847. There is no mention of this sketch in the other notebook of field notes, nor of Kane's having witnessed the game being played,[53] so this is the only reference to it in Kane's hand. Another sketch made in the vicinity, "Columbia River 50 Miles Below Colville," is pertinent, for it provides the source for the background in the later oil painting; however, it is too faint to permit reproduction.[54]

In the draft manuscript, the game is named twice; in the first instance it is spelled "Alkoloch," which is translated as meaning "(the blue Jay)," and in the second it suddenly becomes the name of the

[51] Divide Ledger D5, 689; Longman Archive, University of Reading.

[52] Stark Museum of Art, Orange, Texas: 11.85/4, [100].

[53] Paul Kane, Field Notes, Stark Museum of Art, 11.85/5, [75–6].

[54] Paul Kane, "Columbia River 50 Miles below Colville" (1847), watercolour over graphite on paper, 13.6 × 24.1 cm., Stark Museum of Art, Orange, Texas: 31.78/77, WWC (Western Water Colour) 78; Harper, *cat. rais.* IV-316.

"second chief of the Schualpay tribe at the Kettle Falls."[55] This piece of nonsense was detected, however, for the name refers in the book only to the game. In the second instance, the name is also spelled "Alcoloch" and appears oddly in the middle of the draft of the *portrait* log. It initiates a description of the game that is barely recognizable as the one described in *Wanderings of an Artist,* where the name is spelled "Al-kol-lock" (*WA,* 310–11). Both descriptions, however, are sufficiently complex as to lie beyond Kane's narrative skills. The book's description, far more detailed than the draft manuscript's, reads in part as follows:

> The two players, stripped naked, are armed each with a very slight spear about three feet long, and finely pointed with bone; one of them takes a ring made of bone, or some heavy wood, and wound round with cord; this ring is about three inches in diameter, on the inner circumference of which are fastened six beads of different colours at equal distances. (*WA,* 310)

Add to this refinement Kane's oil painting, *Game of Al-kol-lock* (Fig. 6), which not only clothes but dresses up the bystanders, heightens the horses into steeds apparently stolen from Delacroix in order to provide prizes worthy of the competitors, and hauls on stage a variety of background items, including an oak which the Forest of Arden is still hoping will be returned.[56] Meanwhile, the horses lose their significance, for the book fails to include what the draft manuscript and Kane's field portrait log mention—that they represent the stakes of the match. Given that the National Gallery of Canada established its collection with this and five other oil paintings by Kane, it is odd that the game is still no better understood. One searches in vain for any ethnological account, and although it is clear that versions of the hoop

---

[55] Stark Museum of Art, Orange Texas: 11.85/3, 63.
[56] A copy of the same picture is *Chualpays Playing at Alcoloh,* oil on canvas, 45.7 × 74.0 cm, National Gallery of Canada NGC60; Harper, *cat. rais,* IV–321; illus. in Harper as fig. 126, 224.

and stick game were played right the way up the west side of the continent, when one looks up Alcoloch or any of its variant spellings in the standard sources, the only descriptions given are quoted from "Paul Kane's" *Wanderings of an Artist*.[57]

This example may also serve to illustrate that the book does not possess the two-part structure of the field notes and draft manuscript. But the narrative repercussions are remarkable, for the editors seldom bothered to provide smooth transitions when wedging an item from the landscape or portrait log into the body of the travel narrative. The published description of this game comprises a discrete paragraph which interrupts a description of the two chiefs who preside over the annual salmon run at Kettle Falls. One paragraph deals with obsessiveness with gambling. Then, preceding the paragraph on the game comes a brief one dealing absurdly with a story of two sisters, wives of the same man, who, without knowing of each other's intentions, hanged themselves out of jealousy for each other. Subsequent to the description of the game is a paragraph describing how the "'Salmon Chief'" regulates the fishery. The game does not appear to have anything to do with gambling, suicide, or fishing, but how the reader only of *Wanderings of an Artist* is to know as much remains unclear.

As to lacunae in the field notes, one imagines the regret with which Edmontonians familiar with Kane's book will greet the news that

---

[57] Stewart Culin, *Games of the North American Indians*, in *Twenty-Fourth Annual Report of the Bureau of American Ethnology to the Smithsonian Institution, 1902–1903, by W. H. Holmes, Chief* (Washington: Government Printing Office, 1907); rpt. (New York: Dover, 1985), 457. A later description of the game, as played by the neighbouring Cœur d'Alêne, agrees in most particulars with the account given in *WA*. See James A. Teit, "The Salishan Tribes of the Western Plateaus," ed. by Franz Boas, in *Forty-Fifth Annual Report of the Bureau of American Ethnology to the Secretary of the Smithsonian Institution 1927–1928* (Washington: Government Printing Office, 1930), 131. This being the case, one hesitates to suggest that Kane or his editors duplicated a report provided in another published source (one has not yet been found); it may be that Kane's eyewitness recollection, unaided by a written record, sufficed for the source in his book. A further reference is François Gagnon, "Jeux d'Indiens," *vie des arts*, vol. XXI, no. 83 (été 1976), 14–17.

neither the field notes nor the draft manuscript reports a Christmas banquet at Fort Edmonton in 1847. This portion of the published account is excerpted almost annually by the city's newspapers for their mouth-watering readership, and quoted effusively by the guides at the modern reproduction of Fort Edmonton. Such a mid-Victorian jollification seems to have been another of the purple patches added once the narrative migrated to London. Regret must be admitted over the absence in Kane's own writings of any source for the memorable banquet scene: "At the head, before Mr. Harriet, was a large dish of boiled buffalo hump; at the foot smoked a boiled buffalo calf. Start not, gentle reader, the calf is very small, and is taken from the cow by the Cæsarean operation long before it attains its full growth" (*WA*, 375–6). Here Bulwer Lytton has found a dangerous rival. An equally unenthusiastic response may be anticipated of the reader from Oregon who counts Kane as one of his region's early traveller/historians, when it is learned that, so far as the field notes alone are concerned, the entire trip from Fort Vancouver up the Willamette River valley in the first months of 1847, an historically poignant date in Oregon history, did not occur.

Finally, to return for a moment to Kane's sketching of the Saulteaux, "Caw-ce-ca.ce che-cock: the constant scie/Skey." In the book, the field note's idiom, "rite thare portraits," which the draft manuscript had enervated to "'write their likenesses,'" is tediously rendered as "take their likenesses." Meanwhile, the introductory "nacad man" of the field note, the "entirely naked" man of the draft manuscript, has fallen on worse times and is now also a "huge ugly-looking fellow," made so by the "Great Spirit" (*WA*, 102) the stereotype of whom is signalled by capitalization. Moreover, the book unhelpfully presents the girl in mourning too simply: "… she refused, as she could not dress herself suitably for such an occasion, being in mourning for some friends she had lost, and therefore only wearing her oldest and dirtiest clothes." The conjunctive adverb "therefore" manages rather to obscure than to clarify the connection between mourning and not washing, so the superlatives "oldest and dirtiest" imply a judgement that was not intended by the draft manuscript (the field note did not mention these qualities of her clothing).

In addition, more in the book than in the draft manuscript, Kane wins the mother's consent to paint "the constant scie" by a sophisticated rhetorical thrust and parry: "... might shorten her life ... more likely to prolong it" (*WA*, 102). When one recollects that this joust occurs through an interpreter, it assumes an absurdity that Kane does not earn on his own. A further change may be only accidental: in the book, the medicine man bargaining fair winds now "hesitatingly" reduces his price, thereby appearing simple instead of realistic. But the final absurdity is offered by the book's re-situation of "The Constant Sky" to a point chronologically and structurally, if not geographically, distant. Two years later, on his way home, the published traveller meets someone now named "Caw-kee-ka-keesh-e-ko, 'The Constant Sky'" at the mouth of the "Behring's [Berens] River," slightly more than half-way up the eastern shore of Lake Winnipeg. Now she is a "Sotto" woman, and she complies with alacrity to being painted under a tree with her child. The single paragraph describing this later meeting bears all the signs of conventional editorial filler:

> By way of passing the time, I took my gun and strolled up the river, accompanied by the guide, and fell in with a solitary Sotto woman and child sitting under a tree. She was quite alone, as her husband had gone up the river fishing in the morning. She did not appear to be at all alarmed or confused at our approach, and freely entered into conversation with the guide, to whom she told her name, Caw-kee-ka-keesh-e-ko, "The Constant Sky." Tempted by the beauty of the scene, and she seeming to be in no wise unwilling, I sketched her likeness and the surrounding landscape with considerable care. (*WA*, 438)

Were it not for the evidence that Kane's oil painting *Caw-kee-kee-keesh-e-ko* (Fig. 7) was delivered to his patron George W. Allan in 1856,[58] three years prior to the book's publication, one might almost be persuaded by its conventionality that the portrait resulted from,

---

[58] Harper, *Paul Kane's Frontier*, appendix 5, no. 59; 321.

rather than sponsored, this purple patch which introduces the domestic dimensions of husband and child as perhaps the principal of its stylizations. In addition to these substantive alterations—more than usual, certainly not "unusually little"—one must contend with the appearance in the first edition (and in no subsequent ones) of an Appendix containing a "Census of Indian Tribes inhabiting the North-west Coast of America, for the Year 1846" (*WA,* [457–63]), informa-tion that Kane certainly did not collect, relating to native groups as far north on the coast as Queen Charlotte Island, which Kane never visited, and for a year in which Kane was near the coast only during the second half of the month of December.

While the draft manuscript explains the book in part, so many other differences occur as to warrant the identification of it as a discrete version of the narrative. More assembled as an omnibus than written as a travel narrative, it has that disorienting "effect of a juncture of intentions" that one finds in ghost-written, heavily emended, and corrupt editions.[59] Yet, *Wanderings of an Artist* continues to be cited for its authoritative eyewitness observations, and, more often than not, quoted in the descriptive captions that accompany the exhibition of Kane's art, whether the original sketches, the oil paintings, or photographic reproductions. This is the case at the National Gallery of Canada and at many historic sites in the West. Precisely because the published Kane is both so well known and known to the exclusion of his other identities, a parallel edition, emphasizing the distinction between two of them (those of the wilderness and the parlour), with annotations to the draft manuscript providing at least glimpses of the intermediate one, seems appropriate and necessary. But more important than reshaping the image of Kane is the potential in a parallel edition for placing on view the structures and politics of cultural transfer in nineteenth-century Britain and British North America, and for making

---

[59] Thorpe, *Principles of Textual Criticism,* 20. It is instructive that the context for Thorpe's remark is a discussion of magazine editing; however uninten-tionally, it issues in a consideration of the affinity between the relations of a traveller and one-time author to a publisher, and the relation of a magazine contributor to its editor.

available the complex of Kane materials to scholars not only of exploration and travel but of ethnography as well.

Figure 1
Paul Kane (1810–1871). Paper print on cardboard backing. Oval: 17 × 12 cm.
Courtesy Royal Ontario Museum, Toronto: ROM 976X85.15.

Figure 2
Harriet Clench (1823–1892), c.1850. Courtesy J. J. Lowe.

Figure 3

Harriet Clench, *A Country Tavern near Cobourg*, 1849. Oil on canvas. 29.5 × 37.2 cm. Courtesy Art Gallery of Ontario. Toronto. (purchased with assistance from Wintario, 1980)

Figure 4

Paul Kane, "Two Indian Portraits," 1846. Watercolour over graphite on paper. 13.3 × 18.4 cm. Courtesy Royal Ontario Museum, Toronto: ROM 946.15.61; Harper, *cat. rais.*, IV-86

Figure 5

Paul Kane, "The game of Al-kol-lock, Columbia River," 1847. Watercolour over graphite on paper. 14.0 × 22.9 cm. Courtesy Stark Museum of Art, Orange, Texas: 31.78/77 WWC (Western Water Colour) 78; Harper, *cat. rais.*, IV-316

Figure 6

Paul Kane, *Game of Al-kol-lock*, c. 1856. Oil on canvas. 45.7 × 73.7 cm. Courtesy Royal Ontario Museum, Toronto: ROM 912.1.65; Harper, *cat. rais.*, IV-320

Figure 7
Paul Kane, *Caw-kee-kee-keesh-e-ko. c.* 1856. Oil on canvas. 63.5 × 76.2 cm.
Courtesy Royal Ontario Museum, Toronto: ROM 912.1.30; Harper, *cat. rais.*,
IV-88

THE GREAT PUBLICATION SOCIETIES

Helen Wallis

> Thy Voyages attend,
> Industrious Hackluit,
> Whose Reading shall inflame
> Men to seek fame
> And much commend
> To after-Times thy Wit.
>
> Michael Drayton, "To the Virginian Voyage"[1]

Of the great publication societies treating texts of exploration and discovery, the earliest to be founded and the most important to my discussion here was the Hakluyt Society. It is appropriate that the geographical writer William Desborough Cooley, a founder and Vice-President of the Royal Geographical Society, chose Hakluyt's name for the society which he founded in London on 15 December 1846. In the *Principall Navigations* (London, 1589) Richard Hakluyt had set out to publish "the maritime record of our own men." His expanded *Principal Navigations*, published in three volumes from 1598–1600, was conceived on a larger compass to include the records of foreigners. He imbued these works with patriotic fervour, as a publicist for more energetic enterprise by Englishmen in exploration and discovery. The historian James Anthony Froude described the *Principal Navigations* as "the Prose Epic of the modern English nation."[2]

Both as chronicler and promoter Hakluyt was the inspiration of the society founded in 1846. At a meeting in the London Library a motion was passed "that a Society, to be called the Hakluyt Society, be formed for the purpose of printing, for distribution among the members, the more rare and valuable voyages, travels, and geographical records,

---

[1] Michael Drayton, *Odes with other lyrick poesies* (1619), in J. William Hebel, ed., *The Works of Michael Drayton* (Oxford: Shakespeare Head Press, 1961), II, 364.

[2] James Anthony Froude, "England's Forgotten Worthies," *The Westminster Review* (July and October 1852, New Series vol. 2, 1852), 34.

from an early period of exploratory enterprise to the circumnavigation of Dampier."

The choice of name and the constitution proposed also owed some inspiration to the Camden Society, which had been founded in 1837 as an historical society to continue the work of the Elizabethan chronicler William Camden, who had been a friend of Hakluyt's at Westminster School. Edward Lynam, the Society's President in the 1940s, pointed out that four of the founders of the Hakluyt Society were active members of the Camden Society, and that the Hakluyt Society's laws followed those of the Camden almost word for word.[3]

It was agreed that the first volume to be published should be Hakluyt's earliest publication, *Divers Voyages touching the discoverie of America* (London, 1582). When the Society learned that an American bookseller was preparing a facsimile edition, this plan was shelved, but with the abandonment of the American project, the *Divers Voyages* was taken up again and appeared as volume 7 in 1850. The first two volumes (issued for 1847) were *The Observations of Sir Richard Hawkins Knt., in his voyage into the South Sea in the year 1593*, edited by C.R. Drinkwater Bethune, and *Select Letters of Christopher Columbus*, translated and edited by R. H. Major. The next two volumes (for 1848) were Raleigh's *Discovery of Guiana,* edited by the botanist Sir Robert H. Schomburgk, and Thomas Maynarde's account of Drake's last voyage, edited by W. D. Cooley. Schomburgk's *Guiana,* according to Clements Markham, inspired Charles Kingsley's *Westward Ho!* (1855).

The most influential of the early members was Richard Henry Major, from 1867 Keeper of Maps in the British Museum. He was elected Secretary in succession to Cooley, and held the post from 1849 to 1858. Major ran into controversy. In 1852 Froude, ostensibly writing a review of the first three volumes under the title "England's Forgotten Worthies," came out with a general critique of the Society's work, complaining of both its choice of subject and the ineptitude of its

---

[3] Edward Lynam, "The present and the future," in Lynam, ed., *Richard Hakluyt and his Successors* (London: Hakluyt Society, 1946), 182.

editing.[4] He referred to "long laboured appendices and introductions,"
and declared, "we have found what is most uncommon passed without
notice, and what is most trite and familiar encumbered with comment."[5] Major thought it wise to ignore the article, but when it was
republished 15 years later in Froude's *Short Studies on Great Subjects,*[6] he was stung to reply. He wrote to *The Athenaeum* on July 13,
1867, and published that letter as well as the following correspondence
in the preface to the second edition of his *Select Letters of Columbus*
(1870).[7]

Major's five edited volumes included *Early Voyages to Terra
Australis, now called Australia* (1859). In this Major entered into the
controversy about the possible early discovery of Australia based on the
evidence of the Dieppe maps, which show the large southern land mass
of "Java la Grande." He argued in favour of an early Portuguese
discovery between 1520 and 1530. The general theme of his collection
of texts made his *Terra Australis* a pioneer study which linked the
hypothetical Terra Australis with the discovery of Australia proper.
Glyn Williams and Alan Frost regarded this as the forerunner of the
conference on that theme (held in Sydney in 1988) and of the accompanying book *Terra Australis to Australia.*[8]

On the question of "Java la Grande" and the Portuguese discovery
of Australia, Major changed his mind several times as further maps
came to light. His first hypothesis as set out in *Terra Australis* (1859),
was, I believe, his best effort. Working on this topic as editor of Jean

---

[4] Sir William Foster, "The Hakluyt Society. A retrospect 1846-1946," in
Lynam, ed., *Richard Hakluyt & His Successors,* 148-9.

[5] Froude, "England's Forgotten Worthies," 38.

[6] Froude, "England's Forgotten Worthies" as reprinted in Froude, *Short
Studies on Great Subjects* (London: Longmans, Green, 1867), II, 105.

[7] R. H. Major, ed., *Select Letters of Christopher Columbus* (London: Hakluyt
Society, 1870), i-iv. See also Sir William Foster's comments in Lynam, ed.,
Richard Hakluyt and his Successors, 148-9.

[8] *Terra Australis to Australia,* ed. Glyndwr Williams and Alan Frost (Melbourne: Oxford University Press in association with the Australian Academy
of the Humanities, 1988), 236.

Rotz's *Boke of Idrography*, 1542, with many more sources available, I have suggested the date of 1528 for the Portuguese discovery.[9]

The Hakluyt Society was from its beginning and still is closely associated with two great institutions, the British Museum (whose library departments are now in the British Library, founded in 1973), and the Royal Geographical Society. The RGS had been founded by the African Association in 1830. Sir Roderick Murchison was elected the first president of the Hakluyt Society and held office for 25 years. During this time 45 volumes were published.

In the choice of subjects particular attention was paid to the activities of Hakluyt's contemporaries. The search for the north-west and north-east passages was prominent. As Dorothy Middleton, the Society's present historian, comments,[10] this was in tune with the interest in Arctic exploration pursued by the Royal Navy in the early and middle years of the nineteenth century. The Annual Report of 1865 stated that *The Geography of Hudson's Bay* (1852), edited by John Barrow, had helped in the search for Sir John Franklin, whose expedition to the Canadian Arctic in 1845 had failed to return. Barrow was the son of the well known Sir John Barrow, secretary of the Admiralty and promoter of naval Arctic exploration in the first half of the century.

Major's successor as secretary, (1856–87), was Clements Markham (1830–1916), president for 1889–1909. In furthering "the *uses* of the work of the Society," he saw that ships of the Royal Navy were supplied with Hakluyt Society volumes on early sea voyages. Captain Nares, commander of the Arctic expedition of 1875, received a complete set to take on his voyage to the "farthest North" of 82° 48′N. He also carried Markham himself as far as Greenland as a guest on board the *Alert*. In 1901 Captain Scott, leaving for the National Antarctic Expedition, received Markham's own volumes, *Narratives of the Voyages of Pedro Sarmiento de Gamboa to the Straits of Magellan*

---

[9] Helen Wallis, ed., *The maps and text of the Boke of Idrography presented by Jean Rotz to Henry VIII* (Oxford: the Roxburghe Club, 1981), 65.

[10] Dorothy Middleton, "The early history of the Hakluyt Society 1847–1923," *Geographical Journal* 152 (1986), 220.

(1895) and *The Voyages of William Baffin (1612-1622)*, (1881).

As secretary and president Sir Clements Markham edited a total of 29 volumes. He had started as a midshipman in the Royal Navy, went on the search for Franklin in 1850-1, and to Peru in 1852-3. His books for the Hakluyt Society reflected his South American and especially his Peruvian interests. A bust was erected by the front door of the Royal Geographical Society in 1921 by the courtesy of the Peruvian nation in gratitude for his services as historian of their country. Visitors from Peru a few years ago hung a garland on the statue.

Markham's prowess as an editor, however, called forth criticism from G.R. Crone, the distinguished librarian of the RGS: "fewer volumes edited with greater care would have served his reputation better." Crone considered the early works of the Society not always up to standard; "it may fairly be said much of the editorial work was performed by leisured amateurs — rather than by professional scholars — mostly men of social standing with a knowledge of languages, or naval officers.... The main object was to produce a readable text, and printed versions were often issued with little critical apparatus."[11]

Notable exceptions as editors were the officers of the British Museum, Richard Henry Major, John Winter Jones, who edited Hakluyt's *Divers Voyages* of 1582 (1850), and W. S. W. Vaux, Keeper of Coins and Medals, editor of *The World Encompassed by Sir Francis Drake* (1854). Vaux collated the published text of 1628 edition with the manuscript of Francis Fletcher the chaplain (BL, Sloane MS 61). He also brought to the attention of scholars the world map of Drake's circumnavigation by Jodocus Hondius, published in Amsterdam c.1595. Known as the "Hondius Broadside" because of its accompanying text, this was ranked as one of the most important printed maps in the British Museum's collections. Crone considered the most outstanding of the early volumes Sir Henry Yule's *Cathay and the Way Thither* (1866).

The first series was completed with the 100th volume, *The*

---

[11] G. R. Crone, "'Jewells of Antiquitie': The Work of the Hakluyt Society," *Geographical Journal* 128 (1962), 321-3.

chronicle of the discovery and conquest of Guinea, vol II, edited by C. R. Beazley and Edgar Prestage, 1899. The second series began with *The embassy of Sir Thomas Roe to the court of the Great Mogul, 1615–1619*, edited by William Foster, Vol. 1, 1899.

To sum up the achievements to that date, we can say that the works chosen for publication were notable for their range and diversity. There was no narrow concentration on British activities, although this was one of Froude's points of attack on the Society: "They began unfortunately with proposing to continue the work where he [Hakluyt] had left it, and produce narratives hitherto unpublished of other voyages of inferior interest, or not of English origin. Better thoughts appear to have occurred to them in the course of the work; but their evil destiny overtook them before their thoughts could get themselves executed."[12] As Edward Lynam reported in 1946, works by Englishmen published to that date amounted to about 36 percent, Spanish works to about 28 percent, and Portuguese to more than 11 percent. After these came Dutch, French, Italian, German, Danish, Arabic, Russian and Greek works, in that order of frequency.[13]

The editions were illustrated sparingly. Clements Markham's cousin Sir Albert Hastings Markham (1841–1918) is notable for adding a special study of an early map. As editor of *The Voyages and Works of John Davis, the navigator* (1880, no. 59a), he produced as a separate pamphlet (1880, no 59b), to illustrate Davis's voyages, "The map of the world, A.D.1600, called by Shakspere 'the new map, with the augmentation of the Indies'." The text is from notes by C.H. Coote of the Map Room of the British Museum. The map is Edward Wright's world map on Mercator's projection which Hakluyt used to illustrate his *Principal Navigations*, 1599. It became known as the Molyneux, or the Molyneux-Wright map because of its similarity to Emery Molyneux's terrestrial globe, 1592. In my paper "Edward Wright and the 1599 world map,"[14] I show that the author was Wright, who had

---

[12] Froude, *Short Studies on Great Subjects*, II, 108.

[13] Lynam, ed., *Richard Hakluyt and his Successors*, 184.

[14] Helen Wallis, "Edward Wright and the 1599 World Map," in D. B. Quinn, ed., *The Hakluyt Handbook* (London: Hakluyt Society, 1974), I, 69–73.

helped Molyneux in making the globe. Another of Clements Markham's texts was Robert Hues's treatise on the globes, *Tractatus de globis et eorum usu*, 1592, which accompanied the publication of the Molyneux globes. The text is edited from John Chilmead's translation, 1638, and was published in 1889 (vol. 79a).

In due course various editors had carried the time limit beyond Dampier (1700). B.G. Corney in 1913 edited *The quest and occupation of Tahiti by emissaries of Spain during the year 1772–1776*, vol I, with vol II following in 1915 (Ser. 2, nos. 32 & 36). The Society ventured into the nineteenth century with *The voyage of Captain Bellingshausen, 1819–21*, edited by Frank Debenham, vols. 1 and 2, 1945.

Sir William Foster summed up the Society's first century of achievements in his essay "The Hakluyt Society. A retrospect: 1846–1946," in the volume edited by Edward Lynam, Superintendant of the Map Room at the British Museum, to commemorate the centenary of the Society in 1946.[15] And turning to "the present and the future" in his own essay, Lynam cautioned editors against being over-erudite or over-enthusiastic: "a true scholar never bores or bewilders his readers." He also drew attention to the remarkable fact that the subscription remained what it had been in 1846, one guinea a year.[16] Dorothy Middleton has enlarged on the history in her excellent paper "The early history of the Hakluyt Society 1847–1923," mentioned above.

Lynam admitted to some omissions. The Society had not covered the periods of exploration systematically: "we have done little justice to the numerous records of travel in the Pacific Ocean, in Africa and in Asiatic Russia in the eighteenth century." He added "the moment has come for our Society to survey the whole history of travel and exploration, to draw up a coordinated table of regions and periods which we have neglected, and to base our further publications upon that."[17]

The Pacific in the eighteenth century was one of the neglected areas to which the Society then turned its attention. The most conspicu-

---

[15] Lynam, ed., *Richard Hakluyt and his Successors*, 143–70.
[16] Lynam, ed., *Richard Hakluyt and his Successors*, 185, 188.
[17] Lynam, ed., *Richard Hakluyt and his Successors*, 187.

ous omission was Captain James Cook. The task of editing Cook demanded a man of special qualities and experience. John Cawte Beaglehole (1901–1971) emerged in New Zealand to fulfil this role. His name is as immortally associated with Cook as Boswell's is with Dr. Johnson.[18] His *Exploration of the Pacific* (1934) had marked him out as a leading maritime historian. After the Second World War he took up for the Hakluyt Society the editing of *The Journals of Captain James Cook*. These came out in four massive volumes, 1955–67, accompanied by a portfolio of charts edited by R. A. Skelton. Many letters flew between Wellington and the Map Room of the British Museum in the course of the work.[19] Beaglehole then turned to the biography of Cook. That volume was in course of revision at the time of his death in 1971. It was completed by his son Timothy, and published in 1974.

For his achievement John Beaglehole had been awarded Honorary membership of the Hakluyt Society. In March 1970, while in New Zealand for the Cook Bicentenary, Her Majesty the Queen conferred on him the Order of Merit. (He was the second OM in New Zealand; the first was Rutherford.) A few days after this event, I was privileged to visit the Beagleholes in Wellington and saw John for the last time.

Malcolm Letts, the then President of the Hakluyt Society, opens his General Preface to Beaglehole's *Cook* with the words, "the study of Cook is the illumination of all discovery" (I, p. v). In the eighteenth century editing the *Journals* had proved the downfall of the first editor, and it was a source of much trial and tribulation to the second. For the first voyage John Hawkesworth had been chosen as a "proper person to write the voyage." In Dr Charles Burney's view, he was "an ingenious writer and honourable man." A "miscellaneous writer," he had collaborated with Johnson as literary editor of *The Adventurer*. He was now entrusted with the editing not only of Cook's first voyage but

---

[18] Helen Wallis, obituary of J. C. Beaglehole, *Geographical Journal*, 138 (1972), 124–6.

[19] Now preserved in the Beaglehole archives, Victoria University, Wellington, New Zealand.

also of the previous circumnavigations of John Byron (1764–6), Samuel Wallis (1766–8) and Philip Carteret (1766–9).

When Hawkesworth's *Voyages* came out in 1773, they proved to be a best seller, a highly profitable enterprise for all concerned. French and German editions were published in 1774, and the work also came out in shilling parts. But the *Voyages* were flawed.

Immediately on publication they aroused a storm of criticism. When Hawkesworth died six months later in November 1773, it was rumoured that he had taken an overdose of opium. Nevertheless, for a hundred and twenty years, as Beaglehole observed, so far as the first voyage was concerned, Hawkesworth was Cook.[20] He also remained the authority for Byron's and Carteret's voyages. Up to 1955 only Wallis's voyage had been supplanted by a new text, the journal of George Robinson, mate of the *Dolphin*, edited by Hugh Carrington, and published by the Hakluyt Society in 1948 under the title *The Discovery of Tahiti*.

Beaglehole expounds with typical wit the criticisms of Hawkesworth's *Voyages*. Morality, theology and geography had been affronted. On the question of morality, the account of Tahitian customs had brought blushes to the cheeks of all the ladies of England. You might have supposed from the press that Hawkesworth himself had participated in the Tahitian indulgences. As for theology, Hawkesworth had put forward daringly unorthodox views in not attributing critical escapes from danger to "the particular interposition of Providence."[21] Hawkesworth saw dangers and escapes equally as part of the Divine order of things.

Hawkesworth's geographical comments annoyed the hydrographer Alexander Dalrymple, who had been disappointed in his hope of commanding the expedition. He professed disbelief in Cook's report

[20] J. C. Beaglehole, ed., *The Journals of Captain James Cook on his Voyages of Discovery*, 4 vols. (Cambridge: published for the Hakluyt Society at the University Press, 1955–74), I, ccliii.

[21] John Hawkesworth, *An account of the voyages undertaken ... for making discoveries in the Southern Hemisphere,* third octavo edition (London: 1785), xxiv–v.

that there was no southern continent. Hawkesworth responded in the second edition with some facetious comments; Dalrymple countered with a second letter which he withheld on the news of Hawkesworth's death.

When Boswell asked Cook, back from the second voyage, for his views on Hawkesworth, Cook replied that Hawkesworth had drawn general conclusions from particular facts, and would take as facts what was hearsay. "Why, Sir," said Boswell, "Hawkesworth has used your narrative as a London tavernkeeper does wine. He has *brewed* it."[22]

Hawkesworth's preference for Joseph Banks's narrative over Cook's plain words contributed to this "brewing" of the text. He incorporated Banks freely, using, however, the first person, so that the two men's minds were amalgamated, with incongruous results. The newspaper correspondence which the *Voyages* provoked has enabled us to add further evidence to illuminate the controversy. Some of the criticisms turned on the nature of the commission. Hawkesworth had gained £6000 for "the easy Business of a few Months, transacted by a Man's own Fireside, whereas the commanders who had made the voyages at the risk of their lives and had written the original manuscripts obtained not one penny of profit from the transaction."[23]

Nevertheless, Hawkesworth's achievement was generously summed up in a letter from a seaman: "I am a Seaman and have a Right to judge of this Performance; upon the Whole I do say that it gives a very edifying and entertaining Account of the most extraordinary Voyages ever attempted, and furnishes a speculative Mind with a great Variety of new Features of human Nature. It may be called a real authentic Account of a new World, such as no European could have figured in his own Imagination."[24]

For the second voyage (1772–5) the Lords of the Admiralty allowed Cook to speak for himself. He was to prepare the manuscript

[22] See Helen Wallis, "Publication of Cook's Journals," *Pacific Studies* I (1978), 170.
[23] Letter to the printer from "Navalis," *Baldwin's London Weekly Journal*, 22 May 1773.
[24] Unsigned letter to the printer, *The Public Advertiser*, 17 July 1773.

with the help of the Rev. Dr. John Douglas, Canon of Windsor.
Douglas, in fact, did much to the *Journal* "to correct its Stile," as he
described it. The style was changed in the process of polishing,
although the matter was not drastically altered.[25] The correspondence
between Douglas and Cook in the Egerton MSS of the British Library
provides evidence of the editorial procedures.[26] Cook was destined
never to see *A Voyage towards the South Pole*, which came out in two
fine folio volumes bearing his name as author in May 1777.

For the third voyage (1776–9) a full journal in Cook's own hand
survived, carrying events up to a month before his death. Douglas,
again the editor, was assisted by Captain James King. On the recom-
mendation of Banks, King was chosen to write the last part of the
voyage, from the time when Cook's journal ended. The third volume,
published in 1784, was therefore King's text.

The day-by-day concerns of Douglas and King are revealed in
their correspondence.[27] They refer to "a *Junto* of Cap'. Cook's
declar'd Enemies."[28] Despite their difficulties Douglas and King with
the collaboration of John Webber, the artist on the voyage, and Henry
Roberts, working on the charts, produced a publication which remained
for many years a standard work on the South Seas. Europeans saw the
Pacific world of the 1780s and 1790s through the eyes of Webber, and
understood its geography and ethnography through the text of Cook's
third voyage.[29]

Beaglehole's edition provided the full manuscript texts then
known, annotated in meticulous detail. Those of us who subscribed in
advance obtained the whole set for £10 – a bargain! The introduction,
written with gusto, brings to life the issues of the time. At the Simon
Fraser Conference "James Cook and His Times" held in Vancouver in

---

[25] Cook, *Journals*, ed. Beaglehole, II, cxliv.

[26] BL, Egerton MS 2180. See Wallis, "Publication of Cook's Journals," 174.

[27] BL, Egerton MS 2180.

[28] BL Egerton MS 2180, ff. 48–49ᵛ.

[29] Helen Wallis, "Conclusion," in H. M. T. Cobbe, ed., *Cook's Voyages and
Peoples of the Pacific* (London: Trustees of the British Museum and the British
Library Board, 1979), 136–39.

April 1978, participants made various reassessments of Cook and his editors. Eric McCormick of Auckland University suggested that Beaglehole's education, described as "literary in the English tradition," led him to see things in terms of heroes and villains. Beaglehole was at times partisan on behalf of Cook.[30]

Dalrymple and Johann Reinhold Forster, who replaced Banks as scientist on the second voyage, were somewhat worsted in their encounter with Beaglehole. Howard Fry took up the cudgels on behalf of Dalrymple, whom he acclaimed as a major figure in British imperial development.[31] On Forster, Beaglehole intones, "but who is going to envy Johann Reinhold Forster?" He admitted his virtues, his learning, but summed him up as "one of the Admiralty's vast mistakes.... From first to last on the voyage, and afterwards, he was an incubus."[32] Forster exasperated Cook and his companions and he exasperated Beaglehole. In *The Tactless Philosopher: Johann Reinhold Forster*, Michael Hoare tackled "the enigma and animus that still surrounds the elder Forster's name." Among Cook's associates Forster was "highly superior in philosophy and genius."[33]

In 1971 Hoare's discovery of the manuscript journal of J. R. Forster in the Staatsbibliothek der Stiftung Preussischer Kulturbesitz, Berlin, added a major source for the second voyage. Beaglehole welcomed the find in a letter to me of 8 June 1971, three months before he died. Hoare gives Forster's achievements their true place in his edition for the Hakluyt Society, published in 1982. As Hoare comments, it is "the journal of a highly literate landsman-at-sea,"

[30] Michael E. Hoare, ed., "Cook Studies: Whither Now?" *Pacific Studies* 1 (1978), 198.

[31] Howard T. Fry, "Alexander Dalrymple and Captain Cook: the creative interplay of two careers," Robin Fisher and Hugh Johnston, eds., *Captain James Cook and his Times* (Vancouver: Douglas and McIntyre; London: Croom Helm, 1979), 57. See also Michael E. Hoare, "Cook studies: Whither now?" 214.

[32] Cook, *Journals*, ed. Beaglehole, II, xlii.

[33] Michael E. Hoare, *The Tactless Philosopher: Johann Reinhold Forster (1729–98)* (Melbourne: Hawthorne Press, 1976), vii, ix.

offering many new insights.[34]

More recently a further source on Forster and his son George has come to light in the German translation of the anonymous *Journal of a Voyage round the World*, London, 1771, which had been rushed into print by the publishers T. Beckett and P.A. de Hondt as the earliest account of the first voyage. A French translation had followed in 1772, appearing, curiously, as a supplement to Bougainville's voyage. The German version, which also appeared in 1772, has been generally overlooked.[35]

David Paisey recently purchased for the British Library a copy of the translation which had been owned by the German scientist Johann Friedrich Blumenbach, founder of the science of ethnography. The text includes a letter from a gentleman in London to the translator, and in a manuscript note Blumenbach identifies the letter-writer as Johann Reinhold Forster. The letter gives details of the first voyage, including the earliest printed account of the kangaroo, and describes the preparations for the second voyage at the stage just before Banks withdrew. It has been included in the collected works of George Forster, published in Berlin, but now must be attributed to his father. We are preparing an article on this new material.

Another important discovery has been made for the third voyage. Lieutenant Commander Andrew David found in the Hydrographic Department of the Admiralty (now Hydrographic Office) "the running Journal" which James King wrote while he commanded the *Discovery*, from Kamchatka to the Cape of Good Hope, from August 1779 to April 1780.[36] The manuscript was tucked away in the Sailing Directions archives. I am editing it for the Hakluyt Society, and shall append selected correspondence from the Egerton manuscripts in the British Library.

---

[34] Michael Hoare, ed., *The Resolution Journal of Johann Reinhold Forster 1772–1775* (London: Hakluyt Society, 1982), dustjacket comment.

[35] The German edition, *Nachricht von den neuesten Entdeckungen der Engländer in der Süd-See* (Berlin: Hande & Spener, 1772), has received no particular comment in the Cook bibliographies.

[36] Hydrographic Office, O.D. 279 MCL 15.

I must pay tribute here to Andrew David's work in the Hydrographic Office's archives. He is now preparing for the Hakluyt Society *The Charts and Coastal Views of Captain Cook's Voyages*. Volume I on the first voyage came out in 1988, Volume II on the second followed in 1992, and the third is well under way. Rüddiger Joppien and Bernard Smith are assistant editors for the coastal views. They have themselves produced the fine illustrated catalogue of the work of the artists, *The Art of Captain Cook's Voyages* (1985-7) for Yale University Press.

While the Cook volumes were issuing from the press between 1955 and 1970, the journals of two of Cook's immediate predecessors were also published, Robert E. Gallagher's *Byron's Journal of his Circumnavigation 1764-1776* (1964) and my two volumes, *Carteret's Voyage Round the World, 1766-1769* (1965). In these new versions we were able to sort out the facts concerning various major controversies. Byron's Patagonian giants, for example, became the subject of international debate in learned circles on the expedition's return in 1766. It seems probable that the Admiralty encouraged exaggerated reports to distract attention from the colony which had been set up in the Falkland Islands in 1765.

For Carteret's voyage, as reported by Hawkesworth, public interest centred on the visit to Celebes. Carteret's treatment at the hands of the Dutch governor of Macassar caused an outburst of indignation. The Dutch documents in the Rijksarchief in The Hague, however, reveal evidence of an intrigue by the Buginese of Celebes to entangle Carteret in local politics. The full story shows that there were rights and wrongs on both sides.

Cook's voyages opened up a new era of Pacific exploration, led by the "men of Captain Cook."[37] Young George Vancouver, who as a midshipman on Cook's second voyage first saw the ice of the

---

[37] "But what officers you are ... you men of Captain Cook," the Hon. William Wyndham exclaimed to James (later Admiral) Burney in 1790, as James's sister Fanny Burney recorded; see Frances Burney (Madame d'Arblay), *Diary and Letters of Madame d'Arblay*, ed. Charlotte Barrett, with preface and notes by Austin Dobson, 6 vols., (London: Macmillan, 1904), IV, 378.

Antarctic continent, and sailed again on the third, went on to make his own circumnavigation, 1791–5. His objectives were to survey the north-west coast of North America and to negotiate with the Spaniards over the disputed territory at Nootka Sound. W. Kaye Lamb, former Dominion Archivist at the National Library of Canada, in 1984 produced for the Hakluyt Society the first annotated edition of Vancouver's journal as revised for publication c.1798.[38] The original manuscript has disappeared, but 25 partial or complete logs or journals by other members of the expedition have survived and supplement the narrative.

In treating the Pacific in detail I have had to omit other important regions. As a contrast to the conquest of an ocean I will mention a major work concerning North America which would have been dear to Hakluyt's heart, D. B. Quinn's edition of the documents illustrating the English voyages to North America under the patent granted to Sir Walter Raleigh, 1584, *The Roanoke Voyages 1584–1590*.[39] The text of Thomas Harriot the geographer and the drawings of John White make this a remarkable record of the earliest English colony on the North American continent, 1585–90. The drawings as engraved in Theodore de Bry's *America*, 1590, became the prototype of the American Indians for some 150 years.

In 1965 the Society honoured Hakluyt with a scholarly facsimile of *The Principall Navigations* (1589), with an introduction by D. B. Quinn, and a new index by Alison Quinn (for which she won the award of the Society of Indexers). *The Hakluyt Handbook*, edited in two volumes by D. B. Quinn and issued in 1974, was designed as a reference guide to the works of Hakluyt and provided a critical evaluation of his achievements. *The Purchas Handbook*, edited by Loren Pennington as a reference work on Hakluyt's successor Samuel Purchas, is due out shortly.

---

[38] George Vancouver, *A Voyage of Discovery to the North Pacific Ocean and Around the World 1791–1795*, ed. W. Kaye Lamb. 4 vols. (London: Hakluyt Society, 1984).

[39] D. B. Quinn, ed., *The Roanoke Voyages 1584–1590*. 2 vols. (London: Hakluyt Society, 1955).

The Hakluyt Society has been followed in the twentieth century by a number of distinguished bodies. The Linschoten Vereeniging of the Netherlands was founded at The Hague in 1909. Jan Huyghen van Linschoten was a contemporary of Hakluyt's, a Dutchman whose travels in the Far East made him famous through his book the *Itinerario* (1596), published in England in translation in 1598. The minutes for the Hakluyt Society's Council meeting of 21 September 1909 record congratulations to be sent to the Linschoten Vereeniging, and the hope that "the two kindred societies would long live in friendly emulation."[40] If imitation is the sincerest form of flattery, it is worth noting that the Linschoten volumes have a light blue cover ornamented with a ship (not Magellan's *Victoria*), similar to that of the Hakluyt Society. The first volume was *De Reis van Jan Cornelisz. May naar de ijszee en de Amerikaanische kust 1611–1612*, edited by S. Muller (1909). Many volumes on Dutch exploration and discovery, including the voyages of Tasman (1919), have been published.

The Champlain Society was founded in 1905, with the aim of editing and publishing works pertaining to Canada. "These publications will be in such a style as to make the volumes a pleasure to book lovers," states the constitution. The name of the French explorer Samuel de Champlain, who opened up the northern part of the continent, was a fitting choice. The *Occasional Papers of the Champlain Society*, Toronto, 1992, offer two interesting discourses: "Documentary Editing: Whose Voices?" by Jennifer S.H. Brown, and "Looking Backward; Reaching Forward: The Champlain Society and Documentary Publishing," by Laura Miller Coles. These emphasize the role of the Society in the development of Canada's culture.

Another publication society in Canada was the Hudson's Bay Company Record Society, established in 1938 by the Company to publish selections from its extensive records. The Society was disbanded in 1983, but publication continues under the auspices of the Rupert's Land Record Society, established in 1984. This society published Richard Ruggles's *A Country So Interesting. The Hudson's*

---

[40] Middleton, "The Early History of the Hakluyt Society," 218–19.

Bay Company and Two Centuries of Mapping 1670–1870.[41] In this work Ruggles describes and illustrates the mapping activities of more than 160 Company servants, together with the contributions of the Indians and Inuit.

In South Africa the T. van Riebeck Society was founded in 1918, honouring the founder of Cape Town, 1652. It produced as the first publication *The Reports of Chavonnes and his Council, and of Van Imhoff on the Cape*, (Capetown 1918). I had a personal interest in Percival Kirby's *A Source Book on the Wreck of the Grosvenor East Indiaman* (1953). Kirby consulted me about the chart the captain of the *Grosvenor* was using on his ill-fated voyage from Ceylon to South Africa in 1782. I found that there was only one standard chart available and that this was based on a French chart 30 years old! The South African coast was marked on this chart two degrees too far west. This helped to explain how the Grosvenor came to hit the coast two days before the Captain expected to see land. Among the other publications of the Society is a volume on *Breaker Morant and the Bushveldt Carbineers*. David Livingstone and Andreas Sparrman are others featured in the series.

The object of these societies is to provide from the original sources a true report of the feats of exploration and discovery, to assess the achievements, to allocate the credits and sometimes the blame (official bodies such as the Admiralty do not always emerge unscathed). The handling of evidence is a type of detective work. So let us commend the editors who chart the tracks through their texts. The publications themselves carry the armchair traveller and navigator comfortably across the lands and oceans of the world.

---

[41] Richard Ruggles, *A Country So Interesting* (Montreal: McGill-Queen's University Press, 1991).

A DOUBLE TRADITION:
EDITING BOOK TWELVE OF THE FLORENTINE CODEX

James Lockhart

When Europeans first came on the scene, most or all of the peoples of the Western Hemisphere possessed a well developed, multi-faceted cultural lore and elaborate forms for expressing that lore. Few indeed, however, had writing traditions. Only the Mesoamericans, essentially the peoples of what is now central and southern Mexico and Guatemala, put records on paper with ink. Of these, only the lowland Maya had ever reproduced whole running sentences of inflected words, and it appears that by the sixteenth century even they no longer practiced the art to the extent they had in earlier times. In the great majority of culture areas on both American continents, not only was there no indigenous mechanism for preserving genres, content, and perspectives beyond the spoken word, but the peoples involved, lacking a tradition of writing, did not readily take to the European version of it, and produced no writings after contact; if a few groups did produce some, it was not during the time when unaltered cultural elements and the experiences of first contact were still in the general consciousness, and rarely indeed was it in their own language. In Mesoamerica, members of most of the major language groups — probably it will turn out to be virtually all when we have explored the matter fully[1] — learned alphabetic writing in the Spanish manner in about a generation and began to use the technique to produce records of various kinds, some in preconquest genres, some in Spanish-style genres much affected by their own traditions. Among these groups the Nahuas of central Mexico stood out, not because their writing tradition had more affinities with Spanish writing than the rest, for the opposite was true,

---

[1] My doctoral student Kevin Terraciano has undertaken a dissertation project based on Mixtec, the language of a group located just to the south of the Nahuas, and is finding plentiful resources. Even the several smaller language groups surrounding the Mixtecs eventually produced indigenous-language alphabetic documents for the most part, though some wrote in Nahuatl as a lingua franca rather than in their own language.

but because they were the most numerous and dominant language group of the whole macroregion and received a corresponding amount of attention from Spaniards of all types.

Spanish ecclesiastics took the lead in introducing European-style writing among the Nahuas. We have only later and romanticized accounts of the process, so we must judge primarily from the artifacts produced. Even with such apt students, the process was not instantaneous. No dated Nahuatl text is earlier than the mid-1540s (the conquest proper of central Mexico having taken place in 1519–21), and for the few early undated examples, no serious recent estimates antedate the later 1530s. Meanwhile the ecclesiastics, mainly mendicants and among them predominantly Franciscans, had been gaining competence in the language, devising an orthography, and working out genres of expression. They operated within the parameters of Renaissance humanism, and particularly according to the precedent set by Antonio de Nebrija's Latinate Spanish grammar and dictionary, as well as the tradition of polyglot editions of biblical and other texts.

But the clerics were not alone in the enterprise, and indeed it is doubtful that unaided they could have had the success that they did. From an early time they took in classes of boys to indoctrinate in Christianity and expose to Hispanic culture in a depth beyond that attainable by the populace in general. A few of the most gifted became the friars' aides and protegés; they often received instruction in Spanish and even in Latin, and in return, in a sense, they were the instructors of the friars in Nahuatl. These aides were the first Nahuas who learned to write alphabetic Nahuatl; as they matured and gained seniority, their influence grew. They became not only amanuenses — virtually none of the corpus of older Nahuatl documentation is in the hand of a Spaniard, even if the Spaniard is in some sense the director or author — but coauthors. They were responsible for assuring that materials such as catechisms, confessionals, and hymns were cast in an idiomatic, socioculturally correct Nahuatl. They provided the Nahuatl glosses that went into lexicons (dominated by the great vocabulary of Fray Alonso de Molina, with a first edition in the 1550s and a definitive one in 1571) and the phrases that illustrated the friars' Nahuatl grammars. They may not have devised the original orthographic model to be employed in transcribing Nahuatl, but in their hands that model was used quite differently than it would have been by Europeans. Almost immediately, Nahuas instructed by the friars branched off to produce documents on their own, sometimes as the clerk-notaries of the new Spanish-style municipal councils set up in most of the local ethnic states of central Mexico in the period 1540–55, using primarily genres of Spanish origin, and sometimes operating even more independently, creating alphabetic (as well as pictorial) versions of their own traditional genres, especially historical annals.[2]

In several instances the friars went beyond the business of replicating Christian doctrinal material in Nahuatl to promoting the production of traditional indigenous lore, primarily with the intention of learning what deviltries they were combating, but with time also motivated by a good deal of simple enthusiastic interest in the topic. The deservedly most famous of those working in this vein was the Franciscan Fray Bernardino de Sahagún, active in central Mexico from 1529 to 1590.

By the 1540s Sahagún had conceived the project of a general encyclopedic history of preconquest Nahua culture, written in Nahuatl under his direction by his Nahua aides on the basis of information systematically acquired from Nahua informants, usually senior and influential. The corpus of material thus created was variously revised, expanded, and reorganized over the decades, until by the late 1560s it began to assume the fully elaborated, twelve-book form of the work known sometimes as the "General History of the Things of New Spain," or more often as the "Florentine Codex," from the best and only reasonably complete manuscript that has come down to us. The Codex itself is a product of the end of the 1570s, and it was not until that point that Sahagún's Spanish translation of the Nahuatl was

---

[2] For a more detailed discussion of the matter of the preceding two paragraphs, see James Lockhart, *The Nahuas After the Conquest: A Social and Cultural History of the Indians of Central Mexico, Sixteenth Through Eighteenth Centuries* (Stanford: Stanford University Press, 1992), chapter 8. My doctoral student Barry David Sell is discovering a great deal about the role of the Nahua aides in his doctoral dissertation project on ecclesiastical imprints in Nahuatl.

prepared; the original and the translation run through the entire work in facing columns, both written by Nahua copyists.[3]

The main thrust of the enterprise had little to do with the Spanish conquest, at least in any direct way. But from the 1550s, or conceivably earlier, Sahagún had been using the same team and the same methods to concoct a narrative of the conquest of central Mexico or, as it turned out, of that portion of it of interest to his informants, who in this case were the people of Tlatelolco, the junior partner of Tenochtitlan at the center of what we often know as the "Aztec Empire." We cannot be certain that the conquest narrative was originally meant to be part of the general cultural and historical survey, but in the end it was incorporated into it as the last of the General History's twelve books.[4] Book Twelve, on which I focus here, thus shares the genesis and principal characteristics of the General History and must be seen in that context.

The history of editing the Florentine Codex bifurcates according to the Spanish and Nahuatl columns of the original. For a wider audience, the immediately comprehensible Spanish part was the whole work, and it has been published without the Nahuatl several times (though the Spanish has not been translated). The deviant spellings and usage of the Spanish version were immediately apparent to prospective editors, who viewed these features purely as errors or defects, and all had recourse to the so-called Tolosa Manuscript, a later copy made in Spain, in which the copyist regularized the orthography and grammar by his own lights, making the text more acceptable to a general readership. Editors have further modernized and standardized following their own tastes.[5] While the bulk of Sahagún's message and even of his

[3] For a detailed history of the General History and the Florentine Codex, see Charles Dibble's article in Fray Bernardino de Sahagún, *Florentine Codex: General History of the Things of New Spain*, 13 parts, trans. Arthur J. O. Anderson and Charles E. Dibble (Salt Lake City and Santa Fe, N.M.: University of Utah Press and School of American Research, Santa Fe, 1950–82), part 1; 9–23.

[4] See Sahagún (1950–82), part 1; 10, 13.

[5] Sahagún (1950–82), part 1; 21–3.

Spanish survives these procedures quite handily, the interesting traces of the role of the Nahua copyists who produced the extant original are lost or submerged.

More serious attempts have been made to deal with the Nahuatl. Sahaguntine scholarship really begins with the work of the German anthropologist Eduard Seler in the early part of the twentieth century.[6] Although ultimately more concerned with the substance of the Sahaguntine corpus and its interpretation than with editing it, Seler published German translations and transcriptions of portions of the Nahuatl of the Florentine Codex, including Book Twelve. Both his editorial practices and his translations are worthy of respect, but I will refrain from discussing them because they bear a generic similarity to the work of his most important successors, Arthur Anderson and Charles Dibble, who through three decades (1950–70) published a complete edition of the Florentine Codex, a book at a time, with transcriptions and translations of the Nahuatl column.[7] The Spanish was extensively used as a source of inspiration for translation, and many passages are quoted for their relevance, but the Spanish column as a whole was not reproduced or translated. Below I will have more to say about Anderson and Dibble's work. Suffice it for now to say that their splendid transcription of the Nahuatl is more than adequate for most scholarly purposes; their translation is intentionally quite literal, but useful for that very reason, and it remains as a resource that any future translator will survey as carefully as the contemporary translation of Sahagún himself.

The Mexican scholar Angel María Garibay, who worked on Sahagún contemporaneously with Anderson and Dibble, had come on the scene a bit earlier but involved himself above all in the philology

---

[6] Much of Seler's philological work is in Eduard Seler, *Einige Kapitel aus dem Geschichtswerk des Fray Bernardino de Sahagún aus dem Aztekischen übersetzt,* ed. Cäcilie Seler-Sachs, Walter Lehmann, and Walter Krickeberg (Stuttgart: Strecker und Schröder, 1927).

[7] Sahagún (1950–82). The general volume of 1982 (part 1) followed the rest by several years, and indeed, some of the volumes had seen a second revised edition before that time.

of Nahuatl song. His main activity with the Sahagún corpus was to publish the Florentine Codex in Spanish, unaccompanied by the Nahuatl, as has been the practice.[8] Cognizant, however, that Sahagún had only paraphrased many sections of the Nahuatl of Book Twelve, and omitted some altogether, Garibay proceeded differently with that book, adding his own new translation to Sahagún's Spanish version; he provided no transcription of the Nahuatl. When Garibay did his translation of Book Twelve, Anderson and Dibble's Florentine Codex project was already under way. Garibay was a highly intelligent, intuitive, but also arbitrary translator; despite flashes of insight and occasional spectacular, half-intentional mistakes, his translations were overall approximately as literal as Anderson and Dibble's.

To date, no general edition combining the two streams, the Spanish and the Nahuatl, has seen the light. As volume after volume of the Anderson and Dibble edition came out, the late Howard Cline began to make transcriptions and translations of the Spanish, hoping eventually to produce a full edition combining his own work with Anderson and Dibble's, so that for the first time both the Spanish and the Nahuatl would be reproduced in the same volume, in facing format, with translations of each. Cline did a great deal of work, but the plan never came to fruition. I have profited from his transcription and translation of the Spanish of Book Twelve, graciously made available to me by his daughter.[9] The transcription is fully diplomatic, as it should be, and the translation is perfectly adequate (translation is in any case a much less crucial matter with the Spanish than with the Nahuatl).

My own undertaking, a volume of the *Repertorium Columbianum*

---

[8] Fray Bernardino de Sahagún, *Historia general de las cosas de la Nueva España*. Third edition. (México: Porrúa, 1975).
[9] S. L. Cline, active in the philology of both mundane Nahuatl texts and Sahagún; see Cline, S. L., and Miguel León-Portilla, eds., *The Testaments of Culhuacan,* Nahuatl Studies Series, 1 (Los Angeles: UCLA Latin American Center, 1984); and see Fray Bernardino de Sahagún, *Conquest of New Spain, 1585 Revision,* trans. Howard F. Cline and ed. S. L. Cline (Salt Lake City: University of Utah Press, 1989).

now in press, includes several Nahuatl conquest accounts, but all of the others together fade in significance and bulk compared with Book Twelve of the Florentine Codex.[10] My one obvious innovation is to carry out, at least for one book of the Codex, a plan like that envisioned by Howard Cline, with the Nahuatl, the Spanish, and new English translations of both all facing. In the following, I discuss aspects of transcription, translation, and the treatment of illustrations as encountered in work on Book Twelve, but also in the broader context of Nahuatl philology.

Nahuatl orthography as employed in the sixteenth through eighteenth centuries was based squarely on Spanish values, with the addition of some conventions for sounds not present in sixteenth-century Spanish (*tz, tl,* an intermittent *h* for glottal stop). Despite an underlying uniformity and ready mutual intelligibility, the various subtraditions that were present from the beginning never coalesced entirely into a single orthographic model, not even among the Spanish ecclesiastics who originated the system, and far less among the Nahuas who mainly practiced it. Spelling often followed pronunciation closely; thus one will find evidence of such things as lenition (*meztli* instead of *metztli,* "month," indicating the weakening of an affricate to a sibilant before a consonant), assimilation (*huelloquichiuh* instead of *huel oquichiuh* for "he really did it," indicating the incorporation of the word *huel* into the nuclear phrase), and variant word forms (*chipochitl* instead of *ichpochtli,* "maiden"). Examples like these tell us much about speech, syntax, and regional variation.

Moreover, change in the system took place across time. At first, the main representations of prevocalic [w] were *u* and *v,* with *hu* as a relatively little used third possibility. By the late sixteenth century, *hu* had displaced the others, to the point that later writers sometimes failed to understand the intention of earlier *u* and *v,* making serious errors of transcription in dealing with texts containing them. Thus on the one

---

[10] James Lockhart, ed., *We People Here: Nahuatl Accounts of the Conquest of Mexico* (forthcoming, University of California Press). The introduction and notes to this publication deal in greater depth with many of the matters discussed here; it is also true that I address several themes more directly here.

hand there is no dominant model which present-day readers would understand better than any other and which therefore would have priority as a basis for modern transcriptions; on the other hand a strictly diplomatic transcription contains essential clues about a given text's dating, regional origin, and intellectual lineage.

Nevertheless, the transcriptions made by modern scholars, especially in Mexico where most work was being done until recent decades, were at first usually standardized in a method based on modern Spanish orthography. The main features varying from original practice were the use of *z* before back vowels instead of the original *ç* (and the *s* which succeeded it in the eighteenth century) and a uniform *hu* for prevocalic [w], although vowels were also standardized, and other liberties were taken. This system became orthodox in Mexico with the work of Garibay, and was followed by Miguel León-Portilla and Fernando Horcasitas.[11] During the 1980s, the philosophy of transcription among the Mexicans, perhaps affected by the work of Anderson and Dibble, whom I will discuss next, began to veer in the direction of a more exact reproduction of the original; the transcription in León-Portilla's edition of Sahagún's *Coloquios*, for example, is fully diplomatic.[12]

---

[11] As in Angel María Garibay K., *Poesía náhuatl*, 3 vols. (México: Universidad Nacional Autónoma de México, 1964–8); Miguel León-Portilla, *La filosofía náhuatl estudiada en sus fuentes* (México: Instituto Indigenista Interamericano, 1956); Fernando Horcasitas, *El teatro náhuatl*. México: Universidad Nacional Autónoma de México, 1974. The latter, however, is laudably inconsistent; Horcasitas left many especially interesting deviant forms as they are in the original.

[12] Fray Bernardino de Sahagún, *Coloquios y doctrina cristiana*. Ed. Miguel León-Portilla (México: Universidad Nacional Autónoma de México, 1986). It is interesting that although Luis Reyes, a giant of Nahuatl philology, is highly progressive and greatly concerned with approaching ever closer to an appreciation of the originals in every way, he and his followers have retained elements of the older policy. (He uses *z* in the orthodox Mexican fashion; he has changed *hu*, but standardizes with *u* instead.) See Paul Kirchhoff, Lina Odena Güemes, and Luis Reyes García, eds., *Historia tolteca-chichimeca* (México: Instituto Nacional de Antropología e Historia, 1976); and Eustaquio

Anderson and Dibble decided to reproduce all letters and diacritics as exactly as typographic techniques will permit, and their policy has gradually become the normal one for scholars working with older Nahuatl texts. It is also my own practice. Here I wish to discuss briefly some of the implications and ambiguities involved with transcribing the Nahuatl of Book Twelve in particular.

Sixteenth-century Spanish script as employed by ecclesiastics used a standard set of scribal abbreviations well known to those who work with late medieval and early modern Latin, to indicate *qui, que,* and *qua*; among secular writers, the only such sign in common use was a more cursive version of the one for *que*. In time, the same came to be true of writing by Nahuatl speakers, but since the first generation writers were mainly trained by Spanish ecclesiastics, the *q* diacritics tend to be prominent in the texts they produced. These signs are thus a prime measure of the proximity or distance of ecclesiastical influence. Not even all the ecclesiastics used the diacritics in the same way. Thus the aides of Sahagún, in whom he instilled a uniform model, hardly used the *qua* sign at all. Some writers in the Tlaxcalan region at the same time, however, made very liberal use of it. The differences reveal the existence of and even, to an extent, delineate sub-traditions and regional schools; hence the original marking must be carefully preserved in an edition.

A major diagnostic characteristic of Sahagún's system in contradistinction to all others is the use of *o* and *ho* for [w] in preference to the other variants (though they appear too). It is especially important, then, to reproduce these quasi-deviant *o*'s, but it becomes rather difficult because in both Sahagún's system and in Nahuatl phonology a clear difference between the value and function of *o, u,* and *v* is lacking, leading the copyists to merge them visually to the point of indistinguishability, especially *o* and *v*. Many cases are uncontroversial, but at a certain point, arbitrary decisions become necessary; direct representation reaches its limits, and only by comments in the

Celestino Solís, Armando Valencia R., and Constantino Medina Lima, eds., *Actas del cabildo de Tlaxcala, 1547–1567* (México: Archivo General de la Nación, 1985).

apparatus can one apprise the reader of important surface aspects of the original.

Much the same thing happens with punctuation. In many Nahuatl texts, punctuation is so sparing that one must seriously suspect a punctuation-like mark of being an error, and transcriptions of mundane documents often, without notable loss, ignore punctuation altogether. Not so in texts produced under the auspices of Spanish ecclesiastics, who set value on punctuation, although their practices were loose and not those of today, and their students seem not to have fully understood their instruction in this respect in any case. The particular way of using punctuation in a text of this type is a clue to its provenance and tradition, as well as to the divisions of Nahuatl syntax. The distinctions between comma, semicolon, colon, and period seem to have sat lightly on the Nahuas (and even on their instructors); all of the marks seem to have the same primary function, that of indicating the beginning and end of phonological phrases. As a result, the writers were not much concerned with externally distinguishing a comma from a period, or a semicolon from a colon; arbitrariness and commentary again become necessary.[13]

In general, then, I advocate following the original as closely as is possible in a printed book, trying to avoid the loss of distinctions of great potential use to research in various kinds of cultural and linguistic history. The one area where I have departed from that principle is in the spacing of letters on the page. In my edition, as in similar publications I have been involved in, I respaced everything into words by modern grammatical criteria. Such has come to be the general

---

[13] A special problem is a mark in Book Twelve looking rather like a question mark, a theory confirmed by the fact that it often coincides with the end of a direct question. It also appears in connection with indirect questions, however, and more notably, with statements of the kind associated with exclamation marks and with other sentences where its presence is rather hard to explain except by the presumption that the writer thought of it as something like quotation marks, to be used with any direct speech by the characters. In the end I used question marks except for the cases where exclamation marks seemed more appropriate, explaining myself in the apparatus.

practice in reproducing older Nahuatl, on the grounds that it is empirically virtually impossible to distinguish spaced from connected elements. Spaces in any case are better called gaps or intervals; the *space* as we know it in a printed book or a typed page was not a part of the script of most sixteenth-century writers, any more than it was of the practice in Roman inscriptions. Ecclesiastical writers, however, did tend to leave a discernible and meaningful space between words, and some of their Nahua students at first did somewhat the same, although the entity comparable to the word in European languages is rather larger, more flexible, and more complex. In the Florentine Codex, spaces are exceptionally regular and potentially significant (articles and some small particles are often integrated spatially into the larger word). Nevertheless, the system falls far short of consistency, and above all, no hyphens were placed at the ends of lines, so that deciding between a space and a continuation at the thousands of line breaks occurring in a small-column format is entirely arbitrary. Anderson and Dibble followed the apparent spacing closely, making their own deductions at line breaks and arbitrarily separating articles and the like from larger words. Their procedure is very reasonable, but since the user of their edition would still have to consult a facsimile to ascertain the full details of the original spacing, I decided to respace even in this auspicious environment.

One must also consider the matter of spacing larger elements. The Florentine Codex in general and Book Twelve in particular are divided into titled and numbered chapters. Although it is clear that the chapter division is later than the generation of the Nahuatl text, it seems better to leave the chapters as they are than to attempt the tricky business of establishing prior units. The chapters are essentially undivided internally in both Spanish and English, except for gaps made necessary by pictures or by differences in the length of the two columns. On purely intellectual grounds, there is no doubt that the surface unity of the chapters should be retained. In fact, however, the modern reader is extraordinarily unhappy with such a solution. Using introductory particles and speaker changes as clues, as have my predecessors, I divided the chapters into paragraph-sized chunks in both Nahuatl and Spanish, loudly warning the reader in the apparatus that these divisions are for convenience only and do not correspond to the original. Perhaps future editors of such materials will have the courage I lacked and will let chapters run on undivided.

The existence of a facsimile thus becomes a prime desideratum even though one does everything in an edition to make consulting it unnecessary. A marvelous color facsimile of the Florentine Codex was published some years back, and serious scholars will consult it regularly over and above any edition.[14] The kind of fidelity on the printed page that I have been advocating, however, is not rendered superfluous by a fine facsimile; printed pages with the relevant details scan far more readily than the originals, not only for neophytes but for trained and experienced scholars, and work with a whole corpus of texts becomes nearly impossible without sophisticated editions at once following and clarifying the originals.

I have been speaking primarily of the Nahuatl text. The transcription of the Spanish text obeys the same imperatives, and is all in all markedly less problematic. One does, however, face the matter of the notable deviance from normal Spanish orthography and even style caused by the fact that the copyists were native speakers of Nahuatl, not Spanish. I never had any doubt that the deviance, being among the most interesting and significant features of the Spanish text, should be preserved (though some Romance philologists apprised of the project were initially of the opinion that standard forms should be inserted in brackets, with the odd forms relegated to notes). The question was not so much the reproduction as the explanation of the phenomena, in order to avoid the impression, dominant until now, that the Spanish text of Book Twelve (and of the whole Florentine Codex) was simply an inferior and erroneous version.

The orthographic deviances are of two types, visual and aural. The latter are more common and perhaps more informative, but the former have their interest as well. We can tell that a deviance is visual when there is no similiarity between the sounds of the standard letter and the one substituted, with the similar appearance of the letters on a written

---

[14] Fray Bernardino de Sahagún, *Códice Florentino*. El Manuscrito 218–220 de la colección Palatina de la Biblioteca Medicea Laurenziana. Facsimile edition (Florence: Giunti Barbera and the Archivo General de la Nación, 1979).

page remaining as the explanation. Thus the copyist of the Spanish once put "se desperauā" where the original intention, reflected in the Nahuatl, was clearly "se despeñauā" "they hurled themselves off." The repetition of such examples (there are perhaps a dozen in the manuscript) first tells us that the Florentine Codex as we know it rests on a previous written version, not directly on Sahagún's dictation (which still remains the most likely ultimate origin), and second it shows us the limits of the copyist's comprehension of Spanish, thereby measuring one aspect of indigenous acculturation.

More frequent in Book Twelve are phonologically based letter substitutions, depending on the similarity of a sound in Spanish to one in Nahuatl. These tell us of how the copyist, and presumably his peers, pronounced Spanish; we can deduce from the relatively frequent substitutions that he had made little if any phonological adjustment to Spanish, using the closest Nahuatl equivalent where a Spanish sound was missing in his mother tongue. Nahuatl lacked voiced stops, thus Nahuas often substituted the corresponding unvoiced stop; lacking [r], they substituted [l], and their lack of a distinction between [o] and [u] led to the merging of those Spanish sounds; the same happened with unstressed [e] and [i]. Since the Nahuas perceived no difference between these pairs of sounds, on the written page they engaged not only in primary substitution, such as *p* (labial unvoiced stop) for *b* (labial voiced stop), but also in hypercorrection, as in *b* for *p*. These phenomena are well attested in the mundane Nahuatl documentation of the time.[15] The bulk of the "misspellings" in Book Twelve are expectable substitutions at the time when they were written, and they betray the fact that even the highly educated aides of Sahagún did not escape the general processes of language evolution. The following table of examples from Book Twelve can illustrate:

---

[15] See Lockhart, *The Nahuas After the Conquest,* chapters 7 and 8.

Letter Substitutions in the Spanish
of the Florentine Codex, Book Twelve

normal substitutions:
p for b: supita for subita (súbita) "sudden, unexpected"
t for d: moternas for modernas "modern"
c for g: delcadas for delgadas "slim"

hypercorrections:
b for p: bueblo for pueblo "settlement"
d for t: desde for deste "of this"
r for l: abrir for abril "April"

o and u:
o for u: arcaboceros for arcabuceros "harquebusiers"
        yocatan for yucatan "Yucatan"
u for o: su pena for so pena "under penalty"
        estamus for estamos "we are"

e and i (unstressed):
e for i: se rendieron for se rindieron "they surrendered"
i for e: los siguian for los seguian "they followed them"

Not all of the oddities of the Spanish are phonological. One will notice that in the great majority of cases, the copyist writes *los* for the plural indirect object as well as for the direct object. Here we have not a merging of the sounds [o] and [e] but a reflection of the fact that Nahuatl makes no distinction between direct and indirect objects, and there are some other traces in the text of Nahuatl grammar carried into Spanish. Again, the indicated treatment is not to banish these manifestations from the text, but to explain their significance to the reader in the apparatus.

Moving now beyond matters of transcription, let me say that any translation of a complex text in older Nahuatl done at the present time is inevitably provisional, not merely in the sense that any translation whatever is always in some way for that occasion and purpose only, but in the sense that rather substantial alteration of substance and tone is likely in the future. Precision of translation gains with the increasing size of the corpus being translated and the number of generations spent on the enterprise. The corpus of older Nahuatl — that is, the known and available corpus — is still growing apace, and although a few items are now being translated for the third or fourth time, many more are receiving their first translation, and much of the corpus, including some monuments and even whole genres, remains untranslated.

The main precedents for translating the Nahuatl of Book Twelve are first Sahagún himself as represented in the Spanish column and second Anderson and Dibble (for they have substantially incorporated the translations of Seler and Garibay). The two are very different. Sahagún as the director of the whole original project was in a unique position to understand the Nahuatl text and even to ask his aides when he did not; he also had a deserved reputation as one of the two Spaniards in Mexico who knew Nahuatl best. He did not aim, however, at a full rendering, but as with most Spanish translations of his time, produced something more on the order of a paraphrase, sometimes with his own commentary. The Spanish is usually much shorter than the Nahuatl (the difference being filled with illustrations), and a few whole sections of the Nahuatl lack any Spanish equivalent at all. Even when translating fairly closely, Sahagún tended (for he was far from consistent) to favor a pithy idiomatic translation over a longer and more literal one. So far did he go in this direction that the wave of translators beginning with Seler often failed to see the connection between the Spanish and the Nahuatl and produced a semantically less accurate literal translation in its stead. Recently we have gained even more respect for Sahagún, recognizing some of his faithful renderings of obscure idioms. Doubtless more remain to be discovered, one reason among others why it is desirable to have his Spanish available in facing format when studying the Nahuatl.

As the first English translators of the Florentine Codex, Anderson and Dibble almost inevitably hewed to highly literalistic procedures; moreover, they were encouraged in that direction by the project's original sponsors.[16] A literal translation always has pedagogical value, and all the more so with discourse as complex and metaphorical as was common in older Nahuatl rhetorical practice. By giving element-by-element equivalents of the Nahuatl, it also informs us of the often (apparently) poetic elements that go into stock phrases, of double structures, of the elaborateness and indirection of many statements in a way that cannot be incorporated into a pragmatic translation. As translators of Nahuatl have moved more in the direction of emphasizing the intention, pragmatics, or sense of the text, they have still felt the need for a more literal component in some of their editions. Some editions, in fact, have included two complete translations, one more literal and the other more pragmatic.[17] A good deal of Book Twelve is in straightforward language that will not look very different in translation no matter who the translator or what his premises. Also, with four facing columns already, there was no place in my edition for another translation of the Nahuatl. My translation of the Nahuatl of Book Twelve thus stands in a quite permanent complementary relationship to that of Anderson and Dibble, and students may find it advantageous to have both at hand in working on the text.

As mentioned above, Anderson and Dibble undertook their translation under certain general instructions, including the prescription that the language should be archaic, in the fashion of the King James Bible. They complied, with some private misgivings, silently resisting in some subtle ways, such as often using the past tense instead of the present because older and newer English coincide better there.[18] This

---

[16] See Anderson's discussion of the beginning stages of the enterprise in Sahagún (1950–82), part 1; 4.

[17] For example, Frances Karttunen and James Lockhart, eds., *The Art of Nahuatl Speech: The Bancroft Dialogues*, Nahuatl Studies Series, 2 (Los Angeles: UCLA Latin American Center, 1987). The idea is not new; see don Hernando [Fernando] de Alvarado Tezozomoc, *Crónica mexicayotl*, trans. and ed. Adrián León (Publicaciones del Instituto de Historia, series 1, no. 10. México, 1949); and Angel María Garibay K., ed., "Huehuetlatolli, Documento A." *Tlalocan*, 1 (1943), 31–53, 81–107.

[18] Sahagún (1950–82), part 1; 4, 6.

rather superficial feature of their edition detracts little if at all from its basic value. Anderson and Dibble actually published another version of Book Twelve, without the Nahuatl but with more illustrations, in modern English.[19] The basic nature of the translation remained little altered. In general, a formal, weighty tone is entirely appropriate to portions of the Florentine Codex, but not necessarily to all of it. My own intention is to retain an elevated tone where appropriate, but not to aim for archaisms and not to neglect the original's occasional strong colloquialism and down-to-earth vocabulary. The tone of each translation, of course, is its own, and not an important part of any general trend of the field. I fully expect that many will find my translation of Book Twelve too colloquial.

To attempt to illustrate the relation of Anderson and Dibble's translation to mine, I will include here a perhaps not entirely representative passage with the two renderings:[20]

in iuh quima, in iuh moma, ca iehoatl in topiltzin Quetzalcoatl in oquiçaco: ca iuh catca iniollo in çan oallaz, in çan quiçaquiuh, quioalmatiz in ipetl, in icpal: ipampa ca vmitztia, in iquac ia. Auh in quimioa macuiltin, in quinamiquitivi, in quitlamamacativi: in teiacantiz Teuoa, in itecutoca, in ipiltoca Ioalli ichan.

Anderson and Dibble:

Thus he thought — thus was it thought — that this was Topiltzin Quetzalcoatl who had come to land. For it was in their hearts that he would come, that he would come to land, just to find his mat, his seat. For he had traveled there [eastward] when he departed. And [Mocte-

[19] Fray Bernardino de Sahagún, *The War of Conquest: How It Was Waged Here in Mexico,* trans. Arthur J. O. Anderson and Charles E. Dibble (Salt Lake City: University of Utah Press, 1978).

[20] The Nahuatl and the Anderson and Dibble translation may be seen in Sahagún 1950–82, Book 12 (part 13) (2nd edition, 1975), 9–10; my translation, which may yet change a bit in the final version, will be in Lockhart, *We People Here* (forthcoming), chapter 3 of Book Twelve.

zuma] sent five [emissaries] to go to meet him, to go to give him gifts. The first was the *teohua,* whose lordly name, whose princely name was Yoalli ichan.

My translation:

He thought, and it was generally thought, that it was Topiltzin Quetzalcoatl who had landed. For they were of the opinion that he would return, that he would come to land, that he would come back to his seat of authority, since he had gone in that direction [eastward] when he left. And [Moctezuma] sent five [people] to go to meet him and give him things. The leader had the official title of Teohua [custodian of the god] and the personal name of Yohualli ichan.

   Most of the progress recently made in translating Nahuatl has to do, on the one hand, with a growing stock of well understood set phrases and idiomatic usages, many of them first elucidated in work on mundane documents, and on the other hand, with a better grasp of syntax, much of it the result of a new generation of studies inspired to a large extent by the work of the seventeenth-century Jesuit grammarian Horacio Carochi. Little advance has been seen in the interpretation of individual Nahuatl words referring to concrete things. With the many puzzling terms of this nature in Book Twelve, I relied primarily on Anderson and Dibble, who searched many obscure modern works of reference and also brought to bear explanations in various parts of the Sahagúntine corpus that are not found in any dictionary. The state of knowledge about the vocabulary of material culture is far from satisfactory, and improvement will be hard to achieve. Perhaps systematic lexical work with modern spoken Nahuatl can provide additional meanings.
   This is not the place to discuss my more specific strategies of translation. I will, however, mention two salient aspects. The first relates to a single key term, *altepetl,* referring to a type of local ethnic state, usually of modest size, that was the framework of Nahua sociopolitical organization and indeed of Nahua culture in general. The discovery and increasing comprehension of the altepetl has been crucial

to recent developments in central Mexican ethnohistory. No one English translation will cover all cases of the word's occurrence, or even most of them; yet a single rendering is necessary if the reader of the translation is to be able to appreciate the role of the entity and the contours of the concept. Despite my general striving after simplicity and readability, I decided to leave the term untranslated in the English version, hoping to naturalize it at least for those who are interested in early Mexico (and indeed, the word is already beginning to achieve that status in the ethnohistorical literature). The same treatment, after all, has long since been accorded in early Spanish American history to an equally crucial, idiosyncratic, and even related institution, the *encomienda,* or grant to a Spaniard of rights to an indigenous entity (i.e., in central Mexico an altepetl).

A second noteworthy feature of my experience in translating the Nahuatl of Book Twelve does not in the end surface unambiguously in the translation itself. The original falls into two distinct parts stylistically, a fact that no one seems to have commented on before. The first, a section concerning the activity of the Spaniards before they reached Mexico City for the first time, is in a rather elevated, highly repetitious style peculiar to the Sahagúntine corpus. The second, the bulk of the narrative, concerning events taking place in the immediate vicinity of the informants, is much more straightforward, colloquial, and action-oriented. Comparing Book Twelve with other conquest accounts, I found that the first section has no close parallel there. I deduced that the first part, which has been virtually the only source for the general view of the initial reaction of the Nahuas to the Spanish presence, was in origin later than the rest by at least a generation, with all that that implies. The difference is much less apparent in the translation than in the original. Yet I deemed it to be something the reader must know about, and I felt that a detailed discussion of the stylistic-linguistic facts and their substantive implications was a necessary part of the introductory apparatus.

The Florentine Codex and Book Twelve along with it are blessed with a large amount of accompanying pictorial material. I do not immediately say illustrative material, because in the preconquest Nahua tradition, the most basic elements of a presentation were conveyed in pictorial-glyphic form, and an oral recital (the origin of the alphabetic text written down after the conquest) was an elaboration upon it; thus the pictorial element was much more than mere illustration. The question that arises is whether or not the pictures accompanying Book Twelve retain the traditional role. Apparently they do not. Much of the narrative itself is highly visual and episodic, and in some cases, as with the elaborate costumes said to have been presented to Hernando Cortés, the text doubtless describes a pictorial original. Yet those pictures are no longer present in the form of Book Twelve that we know. An earlier, all-Nahuatl version has no pictures at all, and the ones in Book Twelve in the Codex seem to have been reinvented, inspired by the narrative, thus approximating European illustrations after all. As I mentioned earlier, their most obvious function is to fill in empty space left by the circumstance that the Nahuatl is much longer than the Spanish. The illustrations, for with this background we may call them that, are done in predominantly European style, at least superficially, although elements of the indigenous tradition, even at times full-scale glyphs, are ubiquitous. It was apparent to me from the beginning that the pictorial element should be fully integrated into the edition, as it should be with any early Nahuatl text, in view of the preconquest tradition. The very fact that the old pictorial primacy was giving way to secondary status for the pictorial component as simple illustration is of the highest interest for Nahua cultural history. Because of early deadlines and, even more basically, because of my lack of adequate training in preconquest art history, I was not able to do justice to this aspect. I did manage to get good reproductions of the pictures into the edition,[21] distributed in positions quite closely corresponding to the original, and I supplied rudimentary legends, as well as a brief general discussion of the nature of the pictorial material in the introduction. I lament, however, not having been able to do more, and I hope that future editors of this type of material will bring a higher degree of art

---

[21] To do so would have been impossible without the kind help of the University of Utah Press, which lent out excellent photographs of all the illustrations without charge. Many of them had been included in Sahagún, *The War of Conquest* (1978).

historical expertise to the enterprise of publishing Nahuatl documents. Simply consulting art historians is not likely to do the trick; it is necessary that someone master both Nahuatl philology and Mesoamerican art history of the preconquest and early postconquest periods.[22]

In summary, transcriptions and translations of older Nahuatl are to an extent for different audiences. There is no large group of people who by virtue of their general education can both read the originals and appreciate the translations. Transcriptions are research tools much needed by a very active but still small group of Nahuatl scholars; translations are partly for that group too, but are above all are the only avenue through which a wider scholarly circle can have access to the materials.

A strictly diplomatic transcription serves best. All the elements of the orthography have European histories, but they cannot be simply treated as though they were directly in that tradition. No dominant orthographic model of Nahuatl that readers would be familiar with exists; only the highly qualified will be attempting to read the transcriptions at all. In the special case of Spanish texts copied by Nahuas, not a common occurrence outside the Florentine Codex until a much later time, one might think that they could be treated in the normal manner of early modern Romance philology. But we have seen that the Nahua writer's distinct culture shows through in his "mistakes." In a well established tradition, one can confidently note the intention of a slip or deviance. Here it is by no means clear what the intention is, or whose intention should count. Two different intentions are involved, that of Sahagún and that of the Nahua amanuensis. For me, the latter must

[22] Dana Leibsohn, a doctoral student in art history at UCLA, is such a person. She is presently far advanced on a doctoral dissertation which treats, equally and in connection with each other, the spectacular pictorial component of the *Historia Tolteca-Chichimeca* and its extensive Nahuatl text. An English translation of the Nahuatl is to be expected in due course, although in view of the luxurious nature of the facsimile and apparatus in Kirchhoff, Güemes, and Reyes García, *Historia tolteca-chichimeca* (1976) another full-scale edition is hardly likely.

take precedence. Ideally, one would make separate versions, or at least annotate extensively, trying to divine Sahagún's intent. I have not gone that far in my edition, and not only for practical reasons or because of my own interests. Sahagún's exact orthography is beyond reconstruction (and indeed, given Sahagún's shaky hand, the original was probably dictated to a Nahua secretary in the first place). Since the syntax and usage are at least ninety percent consonant with normal sixteenth-century Spanish practice, it is easy enough for the lay reader of Spanish to approximate Sahagún's phrasing as well as anyone else. The apparent errors in this material need interpretation in the edition itself; hardly anyone can be expected to understand the interference of the Nahuatl substratum. It is only from large-scale, close linguistic analysis of the corpus of mundane Nahuatl texts that we can recognize the patterns.

In matters of translation, the trend has been from pragmatic with the sixteenth-century Spanish friars to literal with the first modern translators, then back to pragmatic and colloquial more recently. There is some need for double versions with many texts, especially since very few readers can recognize words (drowned in affixes) in the original. True puzzles are left after even the most assiduous translation process. Open questions and mysteries must be tolerated. (A copy editor, feeling that my question marks in the translation were excessive, turned them into angular brackets; I would have preferred question marks.) In most serious translations from European languages, there are few enough questions about the primary semantic thrust that those instances can be discussed in all detail, with all possible alternatives. With a complicated older Nahuatl text, in the present decade and any decade in the near future, this procedure would lead to an apparatus the size of the Bible, dwarfing the text. Furthermore, a good deal of its contents would be pure expression of mystification or desperate speculation rather than informed weighing of realistic alternatives. Translating the Spanish of the time, however, even when copied and somewhat transformed by Nahuas, presents relatively few problems.

The edition of older Nahuatl texts is and needs to be a relatively autonomous subfield. Translation and even transcription are an inseparable part of a larger process of opening up Nahuatl texts, very much including mundane documents that might seem superficially to have no relation to them at all. No truly definitive editions are possible or should be aimed for until the process is much further along than it is at present. And yet a very considerable apparatus of commentary is called for because of the extreme rarity of the contextual knowledge required to make certain important interpretive decisions. Ultimately, the entire enterprise of understanding older Nahuatl texts, from the most mundane to the most elevated, is a single campaign. None of the material can receive fully adequate editions until all of it has been worked through as a unit.

MEMBERS OF THE CONFERENCE

Sandra Alston, University of Toronto Library
Joyce M. Banks, National Library of Canada
Mary Black-Rogers, McMaster University and Royal Ontario Museum
Cicely Blackstock, Toronto, Ontario
John F. Bosher, York University
Jennifer S. H. Brown, University of Winnipeg
Theodore J. Cachey, Jr., University of Notre Dame and the
        Repertorium Columbianum, UCLA
Jane Couchman, Glendon College of York University
K. W. Crooke, The Champlain Society, Toronto
Edward H. Dahl, National Archives of Canada
Richard C. Davis, University of Calgary
John N. Drayton, University of Oklahoma Press
William Edwards, Toronto, Ontario
William H. Fern, Westport, Connecticut
Patricia Fleming, University of Toronto
Luciano Formisano, **Speaker,** Università delgi studi di Bologna and the
        Repertorium Columbianum, UCLA
William Found, York University
John N. Grant, University of Toronto
Bruce Greenfield, Dalhousie University
Francess Halpenny, University of Toronto
David Henige, **Speaker,** University of Wisconsin, Madison
Donald D. Hogarth, University of Ottawa
Leslie Howsam, University of Toronto
Kirk and Cheryl Jensen, Los Altos Hills, California
Nancy Johnston, York University
Steven James Killings, University of Toronto
Marie Korey, Massey College, University of Toronto
Ursula Lamb, University of Arizona, Tucson
Richard Landon, Thomas Fisher Rare Book Library, University of
        Toronto
George Lang, University of Alberta
Michael F. Layland, Victoria, British Columbia
Trevor Levere, University of Toronto

James Lockhart, **Speaker,** University of California at Los Angeles and
    the Repertorium Colombianum
Joyce Lorimer, Wilfred Laurier University
I. S. MacLaren, **Speaker,** University of Alberta
Douglas C. Matthews, Champlain Society, Toronto, Ontario
Barbara B. McCorkle, Yale University Library
Randy McLeod, University of Toronto
John Newlove, Government of Canada, Ottawa, Ontario
Rev. J. Ernest Nix, Toronto, Ontario
Philip Oldfield, Thomas Fisher Rare Book Library, University of
    Toronto
Brian S. Osborne, Queen's University
Ted Parkinson, McMaster University
Carol Percy, University of Toronto
Carolyn Podruchny, University of Toronto
Charles Principe, University of Toronto
D. B. Quinn, **Speaker,** Liverpool University
Dawn Linda Raby, University of Toronto
K. Janet Ritch, University of Toronto
Erika Rummel, Wilfred Laurier University
Yolande Stewart, Toronto, Ontario
Sylvia Van Kirk, University of Toronto
Helen Wallis, **Speaker,** London, England
Ronda Ward, University of Toronto
Germaine Warkentin, University of Toronto
John Warkentin, York University
Scott D. Westrem, The City University of New York
Ian Willison, London, England
Joan Winearls, Robarts Library, University of Toronto

List of Previous Publications

1965   *Editing Sixteenth-Century Texts*, ed. R.J. Schoeck (1966)

1966   *Editing Nineteenth-Century Texts*, ed. John M. Robson (1967)

1967   *Editing Eighteenth-Century Texts*, ed. D.I.B. Smith (1968)

1968   *Editor, Author, and Publisher*, ed. Wm. J. Howard (1969)

1969   *Editing Twentieth-Century Texts*, ed. Francess G. Halpenny (1972)

1970   *Editing Seventeenth-Century Prose*, ed. D.I.B. Smith (1972)

1971   *Editing Poetry from Spenser to Dryden*, ed. John M. Baird (1972)

1972   *Editing Canadian Texts*, ed. Francess G. Halpenny (1975)

1973   *Editing Eighteenth-Century Novels*, ed. G.E. Bentley (1975)

1974   *Editing British and American Literature*, 1880–1920, ed. Eric W. Domville (1976)

1975   *Editing Renaissance Dramatic Texts*, ed. Anne Lancashire (1976)

1976   *Editing Medieval Texts*, ed. A.G. Rigg (1977)

1977   *Editing Nineteenth-Century Fiction*, ed. Jane Millgate (1978)

1978   *Editing Correspondence*, ed. J.A. Dainard (1979)

1979   *Editing Illustrated Books*, ed. William Blissett (1980)

1980   *Editing Poetry from Spenser to Dryden*, ed. A.D. de Quehen (1981)

1981   *Editing Texts in the History of Science and Medicine*, ed. Trevor H. Levere (1982)

1982   *Editing Polymaths*, ed. H.J. Jackson (1983)

1983   *Editing Early English Drama*, ed. A.F. Johnston (1987)

1984   *Editing, Publishing, and Computer Technology*, ed. Sharon Butler and William P. Stoneman (1988)

1985   *Editing and Editors*, ed. Richard Landon (1988)

1986   *Editing Modern Economists*, ed. D.E. Moggridge (1988)

1987   *Editing Greek and Latin Texts*, ed. John N. Grant (1989)

1988   *Crisis in Editing: Texts of the English Renaissance*, ed. Randall McLeod (1994)

1989   *Challenges, Projects, Texts: Canadian Editing*, ed. John Lennox and Janet M. Paterson (1993)

1990   *Music Discourse from Classical to Early Modern Times*, ed. Rika Maniates (forthcoming)

1991   *The Politics of Editing Medieval Texts*, ed. Roberta Frank (1992)

1992   *Critical Issues in Editing Exploration Texts*, ed. Germaine Warkentin (1995)

1993   *Editing Early and Historical Atlases*, ed. Joan Winearls (1995)